The Death and Birth of My Mother and I

An Intimate Perspective

Ingrid van Amsterdam

ISBN: 978-0-473-49460-5 (paperback)
ISBN: 978-0-473-49461-2 (Kindle eBook)

In loving memory of she who is.

Proem

Based on daily diary and notebook entries made by my mother and myself this is a personal account of events predecessing certain death and birth. In an attempt to gain a deeper insight into the mother-daughter relationship and the inevitable changes these events may bring I explore the miracle of dying.

Ingrid van Amsterdam

Content

PART 1

Previously

I can't say that I know when it all started, really. All in all, I don't think we really knew each other very well. Yet, if there was anyone who knew me better than anyone it would have been her. Likewise, I was the one who knew her, inside and out. We did have a mutual understanding of unconditional love and respect and I understood her spiritual beliefs. We did not have to agree with each other one hundred per cent of the time and I can recall many times when she would shake her head disapprovingly. But as it turned out, she did not know that regardless of our tense past and sometimes strained politeness, I would be there for her in time of need, instinctively knowing what her needs and desires would be.

Because of our differences I chose to keep my distance for many years. In fact I even discouraged her from moving close to me when upon retiring she decided to immigrate. I knew she wanted to be close to me. I was the one remaining child out of the two children she bore. To the outside world we grew up in what looked like a typical family of four. A husband and wife with two children, a boy and a girl, and some family pets. For my seventh birthday I even got a small dog.

My father had left the family picture twenty-four years earlier and passed away twenty years ago, ten years after their separation. My brother took his own life a year and a half after my father's passing. Hence, I was the only one left. Through a relative I found out how much my mother missed me, although she seemed to have a pretty fulfilling life, at the time. But it must have affected her decision to make the bold and brave move to travel and to be able to live closer to me, I suspect. Still, I couldn't bear her presence for too long or too often as so much water had gone under the bridge. I was reluctant to let her into my life and yet I supported her in every way I could, at that time. After all it is no mean feat to leave your loved ones behind to live on the other side of the world at the respectful age of sixty-five. All the same, she was determined as she usually was. Anything she wanted to do, somehow she succeeded in doing and she was not scared to work for it. If anything she was the hardest working person I have ever met. Anything she perceived to be less than her best wasn't good enough, so it was very hard to please her.

Even after her moving here we still had a difficult relationship. Mum managed to purchase a property closer to some of her siblings. I was grateful for that because it would give her some sort of security. I never told her the real reason I didn't want her living too close, as I didn't want to hurt her feelings. As an excuse I told her that we had been moving so many times and that pattern was not likely to change - just yet anyway.

It wasn't until after many years of keeping my mum at an arm's length that I decided that 'enough was enough' and I should be a lot more forgiving than I had been. Over the years I had been able to bring up the issues I'd had problems with which really affected our relationship. It was a genuine attempt to clear the air. I hoped that she would take some responsibility at least and not just blame other people, divert the conversation or make other excuses.

All those years, Mum in her own way tried to connect with me while at the same time being challenged by some of the choices I made. This would sometimes result in her withdrawing internally and escape by singing or humming devotional songs, shutting off from reality right in front of her. As a parent she had lost control over her little girl who had decided to make her own decisions, as I had developed my own way of doing and dealing with things.

During the last two or three years of Mum's life I really tried to make the relationship work. There comes a time when one has to acknowledge that at a certain age people are just the way they are and are not likely to change. If I wanted to improve our relationship I just needed to accept that, otherwise I might as well walk away. At heart, I still *was* the little girl who needed her mum.

Nevertheless, we lived at a safe distance away from each other, a distance which felt comfortable for both of us. Sometimes just the knowledge that someone is around is enough, even if you don't spend much time together. Thus, we lived our own lives in peace mostly, not really knowing what the other was up to other than during the occasional phone call or her self-invited visits to my place. Those were the times we would catch up with what had been going on in our lives.

Going through some of her diaries was a way to try to get to know the person she was when living her own life. But most importantly I wanted to know how much she knew about her condition, if anything, or if she might have diarised details about her health without telling anyone.

As it turned out, I think Mum was just as surprised as everyone else. By the time she went to see her GP she genuinely must have been concerned. She had always been very health conscious and usually looked after herself very well with pure, unprocessed foods, natural Western as well as Ayurvedic remedies. At the age of thirty-nine she stopped smoking. "That will add ten years to my life", she said at the time. She stopped drinking alcohol as well. I watched her 'magnetise' people at home (I call it magnetic energy healing) but she didn't believe in self-healing, "because then you are in your own energy field", she told me once when I asked.

As I saw from her notes she still used the same infrared lamp for lower back pain we'd had as far back as forty or forty-five years ago. She kept an eye on her blood pressure with her own blood pressure machine. She enjoyed reading and going out for lunches with her friends. She loved gardening and took pride in her beautiful gardens with flowers all year round. She told me that her father, a gardener, taught her how to prune roses, and in turn she taught me the same. She'd even won a few gardening competitions in her neighbourhood a number of years ago. I remember her showing me the article with a photograph of her holding a silver engraved cup, in the local paper. Since living here, she continued to enjoy gardening but also became interested in growing a veggie garden, protected from hungry birds with a net. In the garden Mum proudly grew hot chillies, spinach, lettuce and beans, to name a few.

In her diary she described how tired or sore she would get from time to time after gardening or long days out and about, doing groceries or socialising with friends and family. By this time she was taking painkillers regularly.

I imagine Mum used her weekly spiritual group services as a substitute for not being able to spend as much time with me as she would have liked. She really immersed herself in it and almost drowned in the godliness of it all as if it saved her from the sadness, pain and despair. And maybe it did.

She thought about life and spirituality a lot. In fact this took up most of her life and she never wasted a moment not to talk about it or to teach it to people, whether they wanted it or not. During one of the meditations with her spiritual group she posed the question: "If I am one with God and with All That Is, to whom do I pray?" She penned down the answer given by one of the devotees: "As long as there is duality you pray to God."

My mum loved learning. I would describe her as the perpetual student, although she might have liked calling herself a great teacher, too. She was interested in life and death and the afterlife, and living life as purely as possible. She loved conversing about spirituality and subjects such as cosmic conscience.

Exactly twelve months before her passing, my mother attended her weekly spiritual service where on that evening they sang 'Manava Bolo Radhe Radhe Radhe Radhe Shyam Naam', she writes. It translates as: 'Meditate on the various names of the Lord such as Radhey Shyam, Sita Ram, Panduranga, who is none other than our Lord of Parthi. The very same Lord was the friend of Saints like Tukaram and Namdev'. (Source: *https://sathyasai.us*). It pretty much sums up her later life. She would read spiritual teachings daily and she then she would try to apply what she learnt. Interestingly, she could be ruthless and relentless in voicing her opinions in the process because she couldn't always see that also others had the right to have and express their conviction.

It was reassuring to know that Mum had good neighbours who would keep an eye on her. When someone called her to see if she was all right when they hadn't seen or heard from her for a while, she wrote: 'I probably forgot to text or email her that I am away till mid-June'.

She noticed how her hair was becoming very thin. On the other hand, I always saw how much more beautiful her increasingly white hair became with each visit.

One day while house-sitting she wrote the word 'euphoria' in large letters in her diary. 'I wonder what was this was all about?' I thought. She followed this up with the words 'horse board painting' almost like an extension of the word 'euphoria'.

At the time, she was working on a small painting of a beautiful Russian-style horse on a thin wooden serving tray. Painting was one of the things my mum loved doing a lot. If anything, I just hoped my mum was happy in her life.

She noted that this particular year it was her spiritual group's turn to do Christmas decorations at their ashram in India. Considering she had been so tired lately she got her pendulum out of her wallet and asked for guidance: "Will I go to India?" 'Yes!!!' was the answer. She had told me about this trip. At first she had not wanted to go because she wasn't sure if she was up to it, physically. But encouraged by her devotee friends she decided to go. My mother was a much loved and well respected member of the group.

At a certain point she was not able to join all the weekly meetings or special celebrations anymore because she was too tired. Her weariness seemed to happen more frequently. She noticed that she had more energy with a vitamin B complex, and she would take sanjeevinis, a prayer-based spiritual healing system of little sugar-based pills infused with energy, held under the tongue.

As long as my mum could she would walk along the nearby beach daily, just a few minutes' walk away from her home. Sadly, some years ago she had stopped being able to walk for long distances. She told me that shopping at the supermarket was OK but that was her walking limit, more or less. But after spending an afternoon at a rest home with Age Concern, a charitable organisation dedicated to people over sixty-five, she wrote: 'Walked down and back, no problem at all'. I checked out the venue and saw that the distance to walk one way was about a hundred and fifty metres.

The First Sign and Beyond

On the nineteenth in the same month, she makes an appointment with her GP. For my mum, making an appointment with a GP cannot be taken lightly. She must be seriously worried. She shows the doctor a raised birthmark on her left buttock. He takes some photos of it, and sends them to the hospital. He tells her that he will be able to remove the lump at his practice. She describes the lump as '3 x 2cm wide and about 1cm high, dark brown and black. It might be cancer'.

Six days later she receives a letter from MoleMap, a service which offers skin cancer and mole checks. She calls them to ask when she will have an appointment for her birthmark. It will be within two weeks, she is told. Later, at her appointment with MoleMap some photos are taken of the birthmark. 'Never seen something like that the lady said', she writes in her diary. She will get a reply from the GP in two weeks time.

In between, she calls me to tell me she wants to come over for a few days at the end of the month to join me for an important event. I try to dismiss this at first by saying "it's no big deal" but to my mum the event is an important milestone for me and I understand that she really wants to be there. She asks a friend to join her on her trip to my place.

When staying with me, she tells me about the birthmark and that she will have it removed. I am very worried as this is news to me and ask if she will be able to travel to India in a few days time? After all, she will have to sit on the wound during the long plane trip. She reassures me that she will be fine. I know that arguing with her won't make any difference. When she gets me to transfer the photographs she has taken from her camera onto my computer, I can't help seeing the shot of the birthmark in the stream of photographs and I am shocked. It doesn't look good. I know my mum did not want me to see this photo.

With my mum behind the wheel they are ready to leave.

She confides: "I know another lady who had a birthmark removed and *she* died two weeks later."

I am stunned. This is not what I expected to hear and not what I want to hear, either. In my head my mind goes round at a hundred miles an hour. 'She is going to her guru's ashram', I think. 'She's eighty-three'. I race through my mind: 'She has given me indications that she will be happy with whatever happens. She is *ready* to die. She will be there for a whole month. Maybe she *wants* to die there, at her guru's place. It is a special place for her where she has found solace for many years'. I decide to keep my mouth shut. I don't want to stop her in her tracks, if *that* is what she wants. I want her to feel free, in case she is ready to go. And *I* need to let her go. I can't let her leave feeling guilty because of me. As she drives away, we wave goodbye.

"Have a good trip," I say.

The following day at the medical centre back home, the doctor takes the growth off. In her diary, my mum draws a picture of the area which has been removed. To me it looks a bit like an eye. On the right she writes: '10cm' and underneath: '5cm'. She is given antibiotics and three sheets of plasters. Afterwards she visits a friend and does some errands in town, followed by her weekly spiritual service in the evening. She writes: 'Early in bed. Very tired'. The next evening we talk on the phone and she tells me how her appointment with the doctor went.

"It feels good," she says.

I can only believe her.

In two days' time my mum will be flying to India. She will be away for a month and will return just into the New Year. I try to ring my mum on the morning of her departure. I just want to hear her voice one more time, before she goes. I get no reply. I am so worried. 'What if she actually dies?' I think. I try to get hold of her several times but no luck. I am gutted. When I lie in bed that night, it suddenly hits me: The other night might have been the last time we ever spoke!

I feel deep pain inside, and our whole life passes before me. My childhood, the good times and close relationship we had then. I loved my mum so much. As I grew up we had our challenges, but I found her to be a great friend during my early teenage years and we spent much time together biking and horse riding in the afternoon or weekends. We went on holidays together. Then, life changed and my mum had a major life experience which drove us apart. For the next thirty years it was a difficult relationship. I had much anger and resentment. As a result I removed myself from the situation. It took years to work through our issues, a little at a time but we never became as close again as when I was a little girl. I had gotten to the point where I needed the truth to be told and needed to stand up for myself.

I had matured and, with children of my own, I had become a woman with a new understanding of life. 'I hope I'll never be like her', I remember thinking to myself. Other times I would say: "If I turn out just like she is at her age I should be very happy."

Giving birth to my children also meant a new birth of myself. I had become strong and no longer would I put up with diversion of conversations, changing the subject. Nevertheless, my mother is still my mother. The only one I've got. The pain is overwhelming and in bed I cry my eyes out in grief. It's almost as if she has died, already.

Back from India a month later, my mum is very tired. She sleeps long and often. She visits neighbours, friends and family to give them presents from her trip. When I speak to my mother on the day after her arrival back in the country, she suggests that she will come and visit me a few days later. I feel that this is way too soon after such a long trip, so I suggest to her to wait six weeks and combine her visit with one of my daughters' birthdays.

A few days later Mum finds out that the mole on her buttock is a melanoma and it needs to be further looked at. The next day she records that she feels a bit nauseous and has a runny motion. The day after that she takes her blood pressure: 134 over 84, with a pulse of 68. She feels a bit faint and very tired. She writes a few cards and prepares a plate with small vibhuti packets (sacred ash) to give away to devotees during the evening's service. She feels nauseous.

An avid photographer, my mother has taken many photos during her stay in India. She glues the photos from her trip in a large album. Neatly and clearly in pencil she writes underneath each photograph. She shows the album to all her visitors and takes it everywhere she goes.

She decides to wear a crystal japamala (a string of prayer beads) as a necklace and keeps it on overnight. She has the idea that she has more energy the following day. Generally she is getting more tired now, though. Even after a shower she gets tired and needs to sleep.

A relative talks to her about crystal energy and gives her an angel crystal. My mother will do anything which can possibly help her. She tapes the crystal on her scar. A few days later she gets a lymph biopsy. They take three samples. She tells the doctors what she wants. 'No chemo or radiation, no lymph removal in the groin. Scan is fine', I read. She calls me to tell me about her appointment and what they have discussed. I sympathise with her decision. Another relative recommends Essiac tea, promoted as an alternative treatment for cancer and other illnesses, and Diet Amazon Tonic III, a nutritional supplement suggesting that it can kill cancer cells. He gives her the number of a naturopath. More tired now, she cancels her weekly painting class. From the naturopath she orders liquid iodine and Salvestrol, a dietary supplement said to have anti-cancer properties.

Two days later, with an arrow pointing at her notes, she writes: '-> Started Salvestrol and iodine 10 drops'. Early in the morning I do a distance healing for my mother.

One of her relatives calls her to ask about the treatment she will get. 'Sweet', she writes. Many of her relatives now keep regular contact to keep up to date with my mum's progress.

At the health shop she buys colloidal silver, a dietary supplement said to be used to prevent cancer, amongst other things. The next day she feels she has a bit more energy. She has been more active today. She puts photos on the computer. She reads. In the mail she receives the Amazon Tonic III. It tastes horrible and it gives her a stomach and bowel ache.

The next day she feels much better, not that sleepy. She finds a way to take Amazon Tonic III after asking her pendulum. If she takes 1ml of tonic with 1ml of water and holds it under the tongue as long as possible, then spits it out and rinses her mouth thoroughly, then it is manageable, she writes.

The following day she goes to the crystal shop in a nearby town and buys some small crystals. She tapes them on her buttock for their healing energy. Instinctively, I have a feeling that her visit to me may be the last time my mum is be able to travel. The next day I call her. I tell her that all my children will come for dinner when she will be visiting me. I know they may not see her again.

Mum has been able to organise a couple of ladies who will do her gardening through Age Concern. She does not have the strength to garden herself anymore.

At her next hospital appointment to get a PET/CT scan, my mum is accompanied by one of her friends. Before her appointment she notes: 'no food for 4 hours before the scan; keep warm; radioactive for 5 hours; take crackers with marmite with me'. When she comes home she gives a detailed description of the event in her diary: 'Put hospital gown on. Got liquid in the vein of my left arm. I could feel it go through my whole body: head top, forehead legs etc. In Lazyboy with a blanket I feel cold. After a while called in for more instructions, when they put the colouring liquid in. I feel hot all over, seems that I wet myself but it is not, only the feeling. Radioactive put in. After a while gone through the scanner tunnel. Light lines, spots go through a part of the tunnel. My feet are taped together, my head is taped on the table, a cushion on my tummy, my arms on top with a wide strap tied on top. I could not move anything except my eyes. They made an extra scan from my chest and head. Finished'. She then consumes an orange and mango juice and a biscuit with her friend in the recovery room. Her friend has made her some lunch. 'Very sweet', she writes. She goes home and rests. She will get the results of the scan in four days' time.

The following day I call my mum to ask how the scan was.
"Good", she replies, telling me all about her experience.

The next day she feels feeble. She takes some sugar after lunch and feels much better after that. 'My blood sugars may be low', she writes.

A couple of days later she rings the GP for the results of the scan and calls the lawyer to change her will. She calls the doctor's nurse as they have found some more spots. In a conversation with a friend, she tells her stories about heaven and hell and the jewellery box and naughty Gopi from an ancient Hindu text. She writes: 'Radha Krishna book of love'.

The following day the doctor has the results. There are metastases all over the body: lungs, liver, spleen, lymph and bone tissue. He agrees with the alternative medication she is taking.

"For some it might work, for some not," he says.

She tells him she put a crystal on the scar.

"Very good," he says.

She asks him for home help. He informs her that a lady will come to assess what her needs are.

At 6.30 am, a few days before her granddaughter's birthday she picks up the friend who will accompany her on the way down. Independent as ever, she insists that once they get to the city, she will be driving herself as she 'knows the way'.

They arrive after a seven-hour trip which includes a lunch break at a little village. Some of my children and my two grandchildren are already at my place. In the afternoon we talk about the scan. She lets me read a printout of the result. The report contains a few pages of medical jargon giving a detailed account of the findings. It all sounds so surreal even though the text is right there in front of me. I just can't get a grip of the seriousness of the situation. My mother tells me that the tumours found are about one centimetre in diameter and have been found in the lungs, liver, spleen, groin, bones, lymph nodes and buttock. She is considering immunotherapy and will have an appointment in less than a week's time. Her throat, kidneys, stomach and heart work well and her arms, legs, head and intestines are good. She has a good conversation with one of her granddaughters about her condition and the conclusion of the scan. Somehow this is a great bonding time for them. She tells her granddaughter that she is not the body but the spirit which never can get sick or harmed - the Atma within. Afterwards we talk about Mum's options.

I tell my mum that years ago when she was in her forties she told me that she would turn eighty-four.

"Did I?" she asks.

"Yes," I say, "and when you stopped smoking you would become ninety-four as it would add ten years to your life."

"Oh yes," she says. "That's right. So maybe I will make it to the end of the year," she hopefully continues.

In her diary she writes: 'Now I am nearly there'. We have a good talk. We discuss timing and I offer to stay with her in about two months if I can manage this with my busy work schedule. By then I should have finished my current projects. Keeping in mind her eighty-fourth birthday seven months away from now, this seems reasonable. My mum looks very well. It is so deceptive. She is even able to take her friends to the local swimming pool.

Mum is her usual self at our potluck, vegetarian dinner. Everyone brings very nice food and we have a lovely time. She talks with some of her grandchildren about immunotherapy and cancer and lets them read the report.

The next day I give my mum energy healing for two hours. I am a bit taken aback when I see how difficult it is for her to turn over from her back onto her tummy. It is only then that I get an inkling of the severity of her condition. 'The whole day we have good talks together, no crying or drama but on a spiritual level', Mum notes. She tells me that she hasn't felt like painting for a few months now, and she sounds a bit lacklustre. Her lack of interest seems to indicate likely depression.

I had always seen my mum as a powerhouse with inexhaustible levels of energy and painting was definitely something she enjoyed very much. Every time she would come to visit me she would bring a few paintings to show me. Sometimes I would compare her with the Energiser Bunny from the ad on TV, where the bunny just wouldn't stop drumming his little drum and all the other bunnies fell over much earlier. So it was with my mum.

You would never guess her real age as she was always so super active. Always full of life with the strength of a horse she seemed to have super powers - at least in *my* mind! I start to get worried. We carry on talking and I suggest that we should make the most of it while we can, and have as much 'fun' as possible. It would be a great opportunity to spend quality time together. Maybe we could do some art together. I could 'interview' her so I can write about her life story as she has lead an interesting and colourful life. Both of us could be creative in the process. She could paint, and I could create digital images - I could show her how to use an iPad.

Mum had lived by herself since I left home about thirty-five years years ago. She had always been the one wearing the pants in our family. She was the one fixing the things which needed fixing. She pretty much had all the tools of the trade I could think of, hand tools as well as power tools. Whenever a serviceman would come to do some work, she would be there watching to see how things were done. And she would ask questions so she could learn how to do things herself. She was short in stature, but had the strength of an iron man. Time and time again she surprised me how her strength never seemed to subside with age.

Mum tells me that she may have started to become affected by her illness about two years ago, noticeably having less energy.
"But it could have even started as far back as five years ago," she says.
'She must be scared underneath the brave face', I think.
She softly puts pressure on her tummy and asks me: "What would that be?"
"It's just fear," I reply. I don't really know what else to say.
She quietly considers the possibility. Now, it is almost as if *she* wants to be the child, wanting reassurance from her mother.
As if she has lost faith in herself, hoping that maybe I may provide her with a positive answer, she continues: "It hurts a little bit here. What do you think it is?"
I try to reassure her but I don't beat around the bush either. We say it how it is, in my family.
"Your lungs, I think," I reply.
It is the best I can give her. The truth allows us to get closer. At this point I don't realise how soon our disposition, our roles in the family ranking will change. This is probably where the transition begins.

On the morning of my mother's departure we have a good conversation She says that she has thought about documenting her life story but after much consideration she has concluded that she doesn't want to do that.
"It brings back too many memories I don't want to go through anymore," she says. "I've been there and I don't want to go there again."
I understand. My suggestion might not have been very sensitive. I just thought we might have been able to get closer, like that. But I certainly don't want to trigger traumatic experiences. She tells how she became a fighter. And she never stopped. She was a survivor.

As we sit on the couch, she asks me if she has ever shown me the SOS locket that has been in her wallet for many, many years. I ask her to read it out to me just to make sure she still agrees with everything she has written on it. As she does, I feel

the need to take a photo of her. She looks at me straight in the eye with a brave and encouraging smile. On the tiny folded SOS paper she has written her name, address and contact numbers. There are her old GP's name and address and a friend's contact numbers. One of them died a number of years ago. As her religion she states 'Universal' and 'Sathya Sai Baba Devotee'. Under blood group it says: 'Please no blood transfusions'. On the other side she reads: 'not allergic' and 'no medicines - don't give reanimation please'. Next to it under 'Vaccinations' she lists: 'I Please give vibuthi; II Sanjeevini Energy; III Spiritual healing' and Under 'Sundries' 'I'm vegetarian; Don't give animal food; Just veges - herbs - plant food'. Other remarks state: 'No blood transfusions/painkillers/injections; No organ or blood donor/nothing without permission. Broken bones set without injections when in coma'.
After reading her SOS note to me she adds: "Morphine injections are fine if it's needed."
'Wow', I think, 'this is for real', even if in the back of my head I think that these things couldn't possibly happen to us, they only happen to other people.

It's a lot to take in and all of it is so very surreal because here she sits with me on the couch. She looks like her normal self, and all the time she has been able to do everything. She has gone out with friends; walked; been to the aquatic centre; we went out for lunch; she was able to drive her car, even if her friend drove most of the way…

I remember a poem I wrote, exactly eight years ago. I decide to read it to her as it seems appropriate considering the conversation we had the night before about life and death and moving into the light - a different realm from the physical into a spiritual or ethereal world:

"I'm a Light Being
At the Speed of Light
I travel on my Light Beam
through Time Infinite
and Beyond
Light is where I left
and Light is where I'm going
while in the meanTime
on my LightWay

I Light Up
All There Is
with my Eyes
my Hands
my Voice
my Heart
I Radiate
and Penetrate
the Positive,
the Negative
(as One they Live)
I Shine
and
All my Love
I Give."

"Did you write that?" she asks.

"Yes," I simply say.

When she is ready to leave we hug gingerly and say our goodbyes. We wave and I watch her drive out of the long driveway up the hill until I can't see her anymore.

Back home, she wakes up from a good sleep, the following day. She makes new sanjeevini. On her sore left ribs she applies vibhuti. From the hospital she hears that her cancer is fast-growing, and is at stage four She asks for immunotherapy and a vitamin C transfusion.

I ring my mum to ask if she will get the immunotherapy she inquired about. She tells me yes. I also ask about the vitamin C infusion and the prognosis. She doesn't know the answer to that as they didn't tell her at the hospital. They didn't seem to be very forthcoming with information and it seemed as if she had to drag the answers out of them. It seems that only after her persistent asking they told her that she has stage four cancer. They couldn't tell her how long she has left, 'not years and not days', she writes. They told her that the hospice will look after pain relief. I tell my mum that I will be travelling up to stay with her as soon as I have finished my work projects in about two months.

When a clairvoyant friend comes to visit her, she can see our late little dog lying under the table by my mum, as well as a nun who stands behind her, in front of her altar in the corner of the living room. My mother is doing everything she can think of to get better. She keeps taking the health supplements she buys from the naturopath and the health shop. I give her distance energy healing.
One day, two people from the hospice come to visit my mum. They have a cup of tea.
"I am not looking at a terminal patient here," one of them tells her.
He must have thought she looked pretty good too, and when I read it, I think: 'So I was not the only one who didn't see'. She shows them sanjeevini.
"You are a very spiritual person," one of them says when they leave.
In her diary she writes: 'I have no pain, rub vibhuti if feeling uncomfortable, take all the medication and sanjeevini'.

The following day she records that she is tired and sleeps and is nauseous regularly. Three hours after having dinner she notes that she has thrown up her dinner and feels nauseous.

Two days later she is nauseous again. In the morning she goes to the hospice for intake, and sees the nurse and the doctor. They feel her tummy. It is bloated. They give her nausea tablets and a folder from the hospice. The social worker will come to talk about her needs and care and finance. After her appointment she goes to the tyre shop to get new tyres but they are too busy. Early next morning she goes back and this time she can get the new tyres for the car. I am amazed to read that she still does all this stuff when she feels so terrible.

She takes a nausea tablet at lunch but still feels odd. In the afternoon she has a berry and banana smoothie, which she vomits up an hour later. An hour after that she records eating some fruit: an apple, plums and an orange. She is very sweaty. Later she is able to eat some crackers.

She rings me for half an hour. Almost the entire time she's in tears.
"I am so miserable," she says. "I can't keep any food down." She sounds desperate and continues: "This is not much fun, I just want to die. And I don't want to stay at the hospice. The doctor said that I will really need someone to help me because I won't be able to be on my own much longer. And I am not good at asking for help."

I can hear her crying on the phone. I am taken aback. This is not how I know her. I stay calm and say that I will come as soon as I can. I will just make it work. She is very relieved and tells me how much she appreciates that. She tells me that she has told people that I am too busy and that I have my own life, when they asked her if she has family who can care for her. I am hurt. 'She is afraid that I don't want to be with her, that I don't want to help her', I think.

I know now that I need to do everything I can to come earlier and see what I can do to complete my current work project. My head is racing. I have some appointments to follow up but then I should be able to make it. My teenage son will be able to stay at home; he's old enough at seventeen, even though he's still at school. 'He should be responsible enough to be able to cope', I think, even though I have no idea how long I will be away for. I call my mum and tell her that I will be able to come in eight days. My mum sounds very grateful; I can hear she is getting desperate. I prepare myself to be her full-time carer.

After our phone call my mum has a sleep. She emails me afterwards with her diagnosis. At lunchtime she eats some fruit: a mandarin and a banana. Two hours later she throws up the mandarin. Half an hour after taking a nausea tablet she has some spinach and quinoa. She is very tired and still nauseous. Three hours later she takes another nausea tablet but throws up the meal she had earlier. She has some ginger tea. Fifteen minutes later she notices she is sweaty and takes her temperature: thirty-six degrees Celsius. 'No bowel motion today', she notes. 'No meds taken'. At night she throws up again.

The following day she notes a small bowel motion. She feels miserable. Her friend's husband drops her off at the doctor. She shows him her buttock. She has nausea, and pain in the lower regions. He prescribes her Paracetamol and Prednisone. She asks for a parking card and home help. A friend picks her up from the doctor. She still manages to go to an appliance store and a pharmacy in town. Her friend has made her a big container of pumpkin soup and chapatis. 'It's a very nice soup', she writes. She takes nausea tablets.

I call my mum the next day. We talk about the arrangements I need to make. Somehow I have been able to complete all of my work appointments today so I have no further commitments other than a couple of healing appointments the following day.

Too tired, Mum records cancelling her weekly service and is in bed by 10 pm. The next morning she has to vomit after taking her tablets. Half an hour later she has breakfast which she is able to keep inside.

On my last day home, I do my healings and start to get ready for my trip. I cancel all my future appointments as I don't know when I will be returning home. It could be weeks, it could be months, so I take my computer and my iPad too. Just in case I need it, I pack the document in which my mother made me power of attorney a few years earlier, in one of the pockets of my suitcase.

In the afternoon Mum calls the melanoma nurse who tells her she will have to go to emergency if she hasn't had a bowel motion during the weekend. She might have a blocked bowel. In the afternoon a friend comes with Vibronics cosmic energy, which will have to be taken half an hour before or after food. Half an hour after dinner she throws up and again later in the evening.

PART 2

The Changeover

Day 1

5.40 pm: I arrive. I am shocked when I walk through the door as my mother looks very fragile. She seems to have aged at least ten years in a matter of two weeks since I last saw her. She looks so *little*, in her recliner chair as I open the sliding door. Her face a bit pale, with dark rings under the eyes. She looks tired but happy and relieved to see me. She knows that now I am here to look after her and it will allow her to let go. She doesn't need to be strong anymore. I know that right from the start all our differences will fall away. They need to and it all seems so trivial now. I am prepared to start with a clean slate. 'She is very caring', I read later in her diary.

7 pm: Mum vomits grey-yellow liquid, I note.

9.45 pm: One of Mum's friends from overseas calls not long after she has gone to bed. I write it down so I can tell her tomorrow.

Day 2

00.30 am: Mum vomits again, this time it is clear/slimy looking.

1.43 am: And again - just clear this time.

I haven't slept much and can hardly eat. Early in the morning while I have breakfast, my mother goes to sit in front of her altar and starts singing bhajans (devotional songs). This takes about thirty minutes. While I observe her, I can see how hard it is and how tiring it must be as she can barely bring up the energy to do it. 'She must be desperate for salvation', I think to myself. Maybe she hopes for a miracle.

"That is taking a long time," I say.

"That's all the songs," she replies. "I do that every morning."

"You don't have to. I am sure that Baba knows about you," I respond.

She nods thoughtfully.

11.30 am: Some relatives come to visit. While I am in the kitchen getting tea for them they ask her how things are.

"Very good. She looks after me like a baby," she answers.

I am pleased that she is happy. It is exactly what it feels like to me, too. *I* am now the carer. The tables have turned. My mother has now become the dependent one - not unlike a baby.

12 pm: One of my sons surprises his grandmother with a visit. A few days earlier I had been able to urge him to come up and see her, as this might be his last chance to see her alive. I am glad he made it. She tells him to choose one of her paintings and walks with him down the timber stairs to have a look. Lots of paintings taped in bubble wrap stand stacked against the wall. She unwraps each one of them so she can show him. Sitting on the stairs I watch and take some photographs. Then she leads us to the small art studio below the house where more paintings are displayed. He chooses a painting which she says, represents her life story. I take more photographs.

I make a list of all the things which need doing over the next few days. We will need to send some emails with regard to immunotherapy. We need to go to the bank, and do the groceries. When the doctor comes we will need to ask him about the unusual colour of the vomit. We will need to make an appointment with the audiologist, the hospice and the podiatrist.

3 pm: A number of friends and relatives come to visit. They bring cake, food and even laxative pills. My mum tells me to give one of her friends a healing. I am a bit annoyed because I am here for her and not to help other people. I am already tired and I will need to save every bit of energy I can if I want to be able to carry on for what might be a long time. I treat Mum's friend anyway, standing behind her for at least an hour while she sits in an armchair.

When I stand on the balcony I look at the view and the pot plants she has there. There are some flowers. One of them a small rose cutting with one bud only.
"Make sure you water it every day, then it will flower," she says.
Around the corner is a plastic bucket filled with dirt containing a young apple tree.
"Don't forget the apple tree either, otherwise we won't get apples," she warns me and lets out a little shrill laugh because she is fairly sure she will never get to see any.

My mum is supposed to meet a friend for dinner that night and show the photo album from India but cancels it as she is too tired. Myself, I am absolutely exhausted. I had a long drive to get here, yesterday. Having been up with my mum several times during the night while she's been sick, I have had no sleep. I hardly eat as I simply can't bring myself to put food through my mouth. It just doesn't feel right. The entire day has been extremely busy with visitors. I try to make life as comfortable as possible for my mother and try to cook nice meals for her, even though we never know whether she will be able to keep them down or not.

Somehow I find the energy to draw on my iPad. It gives me the opportunity to reflect and helps me process the impressions of the day.

Day 3

My mum must have thought about her daily ritual of praying in front of the altar and decided that she doesn't *have to* anymore. I am glad because she needs all her energy to simply be.

A relative from overseas comes to visit for a couple of hours. Mum feels sick afterwards but wants to go to the bank anyway to cancel some of her bank accounts. I drive her everywhere from now on. I need to be so careful because I

It's not easy to watch someone who
has always been so independent
become so helpless from
one moment to
the next

just
    part
      of the
    process

am not used to my mum's car. The seat belt hurts her with every little jolt. I try to drive as gently as possible. I manage to get a park right in front of the bank. When we get out of the car, she is hardly able to walk, leaning on just one walking stick. It's an extremely slow walk, the short distance from the car park to the bank. I tell her that she reminds me of my grandmother (her mother) who walked just as slow but with a walking frame. 'At turtle pace', I think. Inside, she tells me to wait in the line and takes a seat nearby. She wants to talk to one of the service desk ladies only so I let a grateful customer go first. Once we both stand in front of the counter the lady asks how she is.

"Not good", my mum says tearfully, and almost breaks down.

Quickly I take over from her and ask if it will be possible to have a private office but it is not necessary. My mother gathers herself and is able to do everything she came for. To make me a signatory on her remaining bank account we make another appointment for the following morning. I silently and guiltily remind myself to bring the power of attorney document. The lady at the counter wishes her well.

Back at home she takes Microlax to relieve her constipation. 'Just overflow', she writes in her diary. In the afternoon she takes me down the little concrete path and steps toward the small garden and garage underneath the house.

"Who would have thought a person can get so exhausted," she says.

"It's all part of the process," I reply gently.

It's the most supportive thing to say that I can think of. She shows me around so that I will know my way around once she is no longer mobile. Later she cancels another dinner we are supposed to have with a relative that evening as she is too sick.

We talk about the inevitable. Mum tells me that she knows what she wants for her funeral. She wants a specific golden sari over a simple coffin.

"Just get a cheap one," she says. A 'cardboard coffin', she calls it. "And no embalming," she adds. She doesn't want an urn or a plaque. "Just spread the ashes over land," she says.

I check out funeral services online to see who will appeal to us. I read out several choices. There is one that stands out. They are local and seem nice people who most likely will deliver friendly service. I know that at some point I will have to make an appointment with our preferred funeral home, and again remind myself of the podiatrist. I also contact the district health board who tell me they may be able to provide home help in about five weeks from now.

7.30 pm: We have dinner, rice with vegetables which she later vomits up. By quarter past eight she is in bed.

Day 4

1.55 am: Mum vomits prunes and grapes.

6.39 am: She vomits again, clear but only a little. I help my mum with all her personal care, and help her on and off the toilet. I can see that her urine is sometimes yellow/clear/pink. I wonder if it is to do with dehydration.

9 am: At the bank when I pull out my document Mum says: "Did you bring that? That is lucky."
I cringe internally because I hadn't told her but reply sheepishly: "Yes, I thought I better bring it, just in case."

11.30 am: Visiting the oncology department, Mum decides not to have any treatment at all. The oncologist, a young woman in her thirties I guess, is trying to convince her otherwise and talks about the potential percentages of success and reminds her that it was my mum who requested immunotherapy in the first place. You never know, it might work for her?
My mum is adamant and says: "No, I don't want any treatment."
The oncologist doesn't want to give in so quickly and calls the specialist in for a second opinion. As we wait for him to arrive, she asks Mum about her occupation.
"Retired," my mum says.
"But before you retired, what did you do then?" the doctor asks.
My mum gives her a detailed description of all the occupations she has ever had in her lifetime, all in chronological order. She tells the oncologist that she found Sai Baba (an Indian guru and a spiritual leader) in 1988, and started volunteering for the hospice in 1990. The oncologist is impressed. I ask her what, for argument's sake, it actually means, if my mum did decide to have immunotherapy. She explains that Mum would have to come into oncology every three weeks and have

an infusion for half an hour. In my mind I go over the trip to the hospital which took an hour to drive and was very uncomfortable and painful for my mum.

My mum shakes her head. "No, no treatment," she says. "I just want to let nature take its course. I have had my life. I am eighty-three. If I choose treatment it might add some time to my life - a year, two years? But under what conditions? It wouldn't give me any more quality of life than what I have now. No thank you."

The specialist walks in, an older man with a friendly face. He examines my mother behind a curtain. He prods around a bit and looks at her spots. "I completely support your decision," he says. "Because if we did go ahead with treatment we wouldn't know for three months whether it would actually work."

The cancer is aggressive and very fast-growing. Mum's body is riddled with it, internally and has visibly spread on her skin also, forming hard dark, almost black lumps. They are painful. Where there was just one inflamed and enlarged birthmark, there are now about twenty lumps. Overall, it does not look good. All I can think of is to make life as comfortable and pain-free for her as possible.

1 pm: On the way back from the hospital Mum insists that we stop at a friend's place. Against better knowing I reluctantly stop off at her friend's. A couple of other friends come as well. My mum is just exhausted, she looks miserable, she can hardly move and is too tired to talk. I have to take the reins and tell her it's time to go. At home she takes Molaxole and Microlax powder and rests for an hour. 'Small pebbles came out', she records.

When I have the chance I go downstairs to do the laundry but I can't remember where my mum keeps the washing powder. I can't find it anywhere. It is nowhere in what I think would be the logical place. I look everywhere but I just can't see it.

When I tell her, she shoots at me from the recliner with a sharp voice: "You just don't listen." She shakes her head.

I am hurt. Here I am, doing everything I can to be with her, to help her. I have left my son behind - I have given up my life for her. It is not fair to argue with her either - I know that. It must be frustrating for her, the way she sits there powerlessly in her recliner chair. For the sake of peace I stop doing what I am doing and walk outside. I need to be by myself. Downstairs I sit on an old blue plastic chair outside the garage, overlooking the small garden. I am overwhelmed and cry. I need time out and breathe some fresh air. I can't handle anger right now. When I have calmed down I search again for the washing powder and find it in a cupboard under the stairs, together with the small lawnmower and all the tools in a white plastic container. 'Of course', I think. I go back upstairs.

"I was outside enjoying the sun," I say when I come back in. I am not entirely lying.

"That's good," she replies, "I often do that too."

We continue as if there was never any tension, earlier. It doesn't happen again.

5.30 pm: She eats some grapes.

6.30 pm: The grapes come out again. She takes nausea tablets and Laxsol, another laxative, before dinner. She enjoys her meal and thankfully it stays in.

I am grateful that my mother's place is only a couple of minutes walk away from the beach. Every now and then, when I get the chance and I know my mum is asleep, I go down there for a walk. It is the same beach she walked on every day for so many years. The sea air is refreshing, and I enjoy watching the seagulls and other birds gather and feed in the water or on the rocks. It is great to feel the sand between my toes, and look at the multitude of shells my mum would collect so often to adorn her paintings. With a cleared head and oxygen through my brain I feel re-energised, ready to re-enter my mother's world.

Day 5

6.35 am: Clear vomit.

8 am: The gardening lady arrives to do some weeding. Mum is feeling tired.

12 pm: She finally has a loose bowel motion after a second sachet of Molaxole. The hospital will send medication to the pharmacy for Mum to pick up.

2.30 pm: In the afternoon a relative brings beautiful flowers and a quiche. We have a good conversation together.

__3 pm__: Mum goes to bed and sleeps for two hours. The relative invites me for a coffee at a cafe overlooking the main street and the beach over the road. I gladly accept the outing and enjoy catching up with him as well as the change of scene.

__6 pm__: We have dinner.

__9.42 pm__: Again, clear vomit.
I go over my checklist. There are lots of people to contact: home care services, the funeral home, emails, the solicitor, the podiatrist and the hospice to get an assessment about my mum's needs. I also need to apply for a mobility parking pass to hang on the rear vision mirror in the car.

Day 6

'Prednisone two tablets', Mum notes.

__9.20 am__: Vomit is clear/slimy.

__11.30 am__: We go to the pharmacy to pick up Mum's medication and straight after I take her to the hospice. It is difficult for her because my mother used to volunteer there and knows most of the people. This time she is in palliative care herself. Because there is nothing else we can do, a doctor tells Mum gently to use cypress oil for her excessive sweatiness. He tells me to put three to four drops of the oil in a jar or bottle of water and dab her skin with a facecloth.
"It will be refreshing and it smells nice," he tells my mum.
I tell him the medication Mum is taking. He instructs us on the medication she is allowed to have for pain and nausea, and which ones to stop. He tells her to get a blood test to check kidney and liver function, and calcium and blood count. The hospice will ring us in about four days to talk about the result and will pay her a visit at home. They are very compassionate.
"We can see you can't travel anymore. From now on we will come and see you," they say.
I feel so sorry for my mum. It must be hard to take. We make an appointment for the social worker to come in the following week.

2.30 pm: Some relatives come to visit. After their visit of almost two hours Mum goes to sleep.

5.30 pm: She eats compote with pudding for dinner.

6.40 pm: Watery lunch is vomited.

7 pm: I give her the first dose of Levomepromazine for nausea, just before bed.

9.30 pm-ish: Mum is unable to get up by herself from the bed. She needs help getting up and to go to the bathroom. She is also unable to get up from the toilet by herself and needs help. I help her in bed and need to lift her under the arms so I can get her body straight with her head on the pillow with her feet more centred. It is heavy. I note that she coughs up some slime.

Day 7

Within a week I have lost at least four kilograms as I have had little appetite and have worked non-stop. I spend as much time with my mum as possible and often pat her face with the cypress oil I bought. It does smell nice and my mum likes it as it is very refreshing. In the afternoon she carefully walks over to the table and sits down. She picks up a pen to write in her diary. I look at her and see how hard it is to lift the pen.
As soon as she picks it up, she utters exhaustedly: "I can't anymore," and puts it back down again.
No further entries are made.

5.29 pm: She vomits mucousy/slimy vomit.

Some relatives from out of town come over for the weekend. It is their last opportunity to be with my mum. We have dinner at the dining table. This is her last time at the table.

Day 8

9 am: I hear a big thud from my mum's room. Immediately alarmed I go to check it out. My mother has fallen out of her bed when trying to get up.

"Mum!" I almost shout.

She just lies there on the floor on her side with her eyes shut. She doesn't make a sound and looks completely limp. Luckily she is responsive.

"My hip, my hip," she says weakly.

I try to lift her up but to no avail. My mother's body literally feels like a dead weight, so heavy. I call out for help. We manage to get her back in bed but even with two people it is extremely difficult. She seems resigned to the fact that there is nothing she can do, but I am shocked that she did not even try to call out. I am relieved I have been able to come up when I did, and not two months later.

10.35 am: I ring the hospice to ask for a rail to attach to Mum's bed so she won't fall out again. With her experience as a night carer Mum had told me that you can get a bed board with a metal handle or rail which slides under the mattress. When I ring they tell me that they don't have one but that I can hire one from a medical equipment company in the meantime. They tell me that I might need to get a hospital bed through the hospice. They will send a referral to the district health board and we may be able to get help in two weeks. Two weeks sounds like a long time.

During the day Mum asks me to ring one of the devotees whose name is on the birthday calendar in the bathroom to see if he wants to speak at her funeral.

At dinner time she wants to stay in her recliner chair and asks to eat with a spoon. I am puzzled as I thought she looked quite capable of eating with a fork. But I do as she asks and give her a spoon. I serve her dinner on a small trolley, and steer it across her lap.

7.35 pm: I note 'slimy/watery vomit'.

Day 9

00.00 am: She vomits a little yellow, mucousy vomit.

9 am: I give her Paracetamol, two tablets.

9.30 am: 'Sevredol, half a tablet. (Morphine)', I write in brackets next to my note. The guests have gone.

10 am: Vomit is now pink and watery.

10.37 am: Again. It is very unpredictable and now just contains mucous.

About 10.45 am: I help Mum have a shower, after helping her on the toilet first. She directs me and tells me exactly how she wants it. I put a rubber bath mat inside the shower to prevent her from slipping.
"Not over the hole," she says, "otherwise the water won't flow away."
I move the mat away from the drain which means it is not really effective in terms of slipperiness. We have a little plastic white stool which she tells me to put inside the shower so that she can sit on it. With much effort I manage to get her on the small stool, after lifting her off the toilet. I turn the shower on, holding the shower head in my hand and wet her hair. My mum wants to wash her own hair. I pass her the shampoo. She does quite a good job even though she is very slow and we work well together as a team. She washes her face with one hand. Then I wash the rest of her body with a flannel. We finish the shower almost forty-five minutes later. She asks me to brush her teeth, and passes me her dentures. Touching a person's dentures has been one of my biggest fears in life but I take them from her without hesitation when she hands them to me. I take a deep breath and clean them with her usual salt toothpaste and pass them back to her.

11.30 am: I give her a second Sevredol, half a table: for pain in her side.

I urgently need a commodity chair (my mum calls it a toilet or 'poo' stool), and a walking frame with four legs which she will be able to use as a shower aid and at night time. The hospital bed can possibly wait two weeks.

2 pm: A relative comes to visit. She brings some food. Together they look through my mum's photo album. I take some photos. She is so precious. When I look at her face I can see how hollow her eyes look now, compared to when I first arrived.

About 6 pm: She vomits again, mucousy vomit.

6.30 pm: I give her an extra nausea tablet, a quarter dose.
As I help Mum walk towards the bathroom I just about cannot support her weight. She is not at all stable anymore and wobbles a lot.
I am scared I will not be able to hold her anymore and desperately exclaim: "I can't."
"I *have* to," she replies determinedly.
'If she can do it, I can do it', I think to myself. I gather all my strength and we make it safely into the bathroom.

I note that I need to ring Age Concern, the medical equipment place, and the podiatrist. My mum tells me to get a walking frame and a commodity chair, both on wheels, a shower aid, and someone to come over at night who "puts you in bed/out of bed". I will discuss this with the needs assessor over the phone as she is not able to come in person due to staff shortage. Everything is happening so fast that we almost don't have enough time to organise anything. I note that I need a bed lever and hospital bed from the medical equipment place, and that I need to talk to the doctor to ask about my mum's nausea and that she now has a 'numb bum', as she tells me.

Late at night as I sit by her bed I realise that in our whole life we have never told each other that we love each other. 'I have to tell her before it's too late', I think. For the first time in my life I say: "I love you Mum."
"I love you," she answers softly. Tears well up in my eyes.

Day 10

12.30 pm: She vomits up half the sandwich she ate for lunch.

I ring the medical equipment place to hire a hospital bed. They will ring me back.

Around 1 pm: They do, and inform me that they will be here with the bed in fifteen minutes if that's OK? '*Fifteen minutes?!?!*' I think. I confirm and rush to my mum's room to make space for the hospital bed. There is a small office which already is crammed full with two desks, two chairs, a set of drawers, a cupboard and an entire wall full of books. But there is just enough space to put my mum's single innerspring base and mattress so I get working! As I take the blankets and sheets off my mum's bed my heartstrings pull. The white pillowslip my mum has been sleeping on has embroidery in the same colour, in one corner. It says my name. My mum embroidered it for me when I was a baby and I remember sleeping on it as a little girl. 'She has wanted to be close to me', I think, slightly but warmly surprised. I see that there is *another* mattress in between the base and the top mattress. I am somewhat amused. My mum has always had a knack for storing stuff.

As I am busy taking the bed apart and start pushing and pulling bits and pieces through the hallway, my mum asks me from the lounge: "Do you need a hand?"
I chuckle because she means it but at the same time I assume she knows full well that her offering help doesn't make sense at all. There are many blankets too so I fold all of them except a beautiful patchwork bedspread made by one of her sisters which I pile on top of the bed in the office.

When the bed guy arrives he rides the hospital bed from the street onto the deck and takes some measurements, realising that the angle from the hallway into my mum's room is too narrow to get it in in one piece and he needs to dismantle it before installing it in the bedroom. Once he has brought in all the pieces he assembles the bed, plugs it into the wall socket and tests to see if everything is working. He then teaches me how everything works. There is a spirally wire with a button on a remote-like device which you can hook onto the bed. When you press the button you can make the bed go up, down, tilt the head, the feet, lift the knees, and back down to straight. It all works smoothly. The bed also has brakes so that it can't move once it's in position.

I make the bed exactly the way my mum had her own so that it feels like hers: I put a sheepskin underneath the bottom sheet. Underneath the sheepskin a laminated A4 with a sanjeevini image for healing. Underneath the pillow a wooden mala (a string of prayer beads). Just a top sheet and a thin blanket on top. So that it doesn't look like a hospital bed I neatly fold mum's polar fleece blanket which she used to drape over her knees in the recliner chair, over the foot end of the bed. It is cobalt blue with a white leafy pattern.

In the afternoon I am able to pick up a commodity chair from the hospice and buy a foam donut cushion from a chemist, which will make sitting a little more comfortable.

As I wheel Mum to her room in the commodity chair she glances into the office to see if I have done a good job because she is very particular and likes everything to be perfect and precise, exactly the way she would do things. I feel a bit embarrassed because as we go past, I know she can see that I have not yet folded the bedspread on top of the mattresses and it looks like a mess. She doesn't say anything or shake her head so I hope she's OK with it. I will fold the blankets and bedspread later but suspect that sadly she will never get to see the tidy, folded version.

Later on in the bathroom Mum asks me to rub some St John's wort oil on her tumours as she tells me that it helps ease the pain. The growths have now expanded. I carefully apply some oil to the painful black and hard lumps as I don't want to hurt her. I am upset to see that they have now extended through to the right buttock. All up I can count about thirty now. When I wheel Mum back to her room she quickly looks up at a small photograph of her late parents in the hallway before entering her bedroom.

3.30 pm: She vomits phlegm.

While sitting in her recliner she gets her nail clippers out from her handbag. The bag sits permanently on the floor next to her chair so that she can easily reach it. First she clips the fingernails of her left hand, ever so slowly. I see how little strength she has left, but she is trying her hardest, and she manages to do her whole hand. When switching over to her right hand, she just can't bring up the strength to squeeze the clippers. My heart breaks. This is not the strong woman I know. Gently I take the clippers out of her hand and help her cut the fingernails on her right hand. I am afraid to cut her and tell her I'm scared. She doesn't say a word. I just can't get over how she has become so weak, so fast. She is deteriorating by the minute, almost. Every day there is a little less she can do.

I look at Mum's exposed bare feet and lower legs and notice that her skin looks dry. I offer to put some body lotion on them. She says yes. I massage generous amounts of lotion into her skin, gently massaging her legs and feet. It is one of the most humble things I have ever done. I can tell my mum is really enjoying it.
"Nice", she says.

The commodity chair is definitely a blessing and a lot safer but still, getting Mum in and out of her chair is almost impossible and proves to be a major balancing act which requires all my strength. In the bathroom she hangs heavily with her arms around my neck while I get her from the toilet onto the chair. I support all her weight. At the same time it is quite an intimate moment and I immensely treasure it.
While she hangs around my neck she repeatedly says: "I love you I love you I love you," as if saying it last night has opened the floodgates.
I can hardly believe my ears. "I love you too," I say.

7.20 pm: She vomits her dinner which is quite watery.

Mum tells me of two other people from the Sai Baba group who are good speakers, just in case the first one will not be available on the day. She also tells me to ask for a bedpan, a caregiver and a bed lift, a crane for lifting a person in and out of bed.

8 pm: I manage to go for a walk on the beach. The sun is setting and it's rather overcast. From the steps down overlooking the bay I take a panorama shot.

Day 11

About 6.20 am: I give her a Molaxole. After the toilet I take her back to bed. It is virtually impossible for me to get her out of bed into the commodity chair and back in bed. Mum is deteriorating every day and can't walk safely.

Around 6.40 am: I give her extra pain relief. With so much less strength to do anything she is even unable to put the tablet in her mouth by herself but she is able to drink. She wants me to get the little stainless steel cup from the kitchen because this is light enough for her to handle. She is hardly able to talk and is almost limp now. The hospice nurse has been so supportive. She has brought bags of stuff I may need such as sanitary pads and sliding sheets. Changing my mother is very difficult but I am able to put her in her undies with a pad inside. My mum has found that the more comfortable way to lie in bed is on her side, so with the help of a sliding sheet underneath her body I am able to roll her over.

In the morning the hospice nurse comes to assess what help I may need. She assists me in the bathroom, lifting my mum from the commodity chair onto the toilet. On our way back to the bedroom Mum glances up to the opposite side of the hallway. This time she glances at her late son without saying a word. I wonder if she is thinking about what is to come and if she will meet her loved ones on the other side. I am almost certain they have unfinished business to address in this world, still unknown to us.

With great effort she asks me to get her most favourite and comfortable top and pants ready for the visit of her eighty-nine-year-old brother. He travelled from overseas especially to see her. She wants to look beautiful, ready to welcome him in her recliner in the living room when he walks through the door. When we get her dressed in her beautiful clothes, the nurse tells Mum gently that she won't be able to sit in her recliner anymore. The one thing she had been looking forward to so much can simply not happen. I know she is disappointed. 'She will never see her living room or any other space again!' I think to myself. It occurs to me that Mum stepped her last steps, yesterday.

The reality hits me hard but my mum handles it very well. She has always been the one in charge and in control but this time she must accept. From now on, all visitors will have to come and see her in her bedroom.
"She may enter end of life soon," the hospice nurse tells me quietly.
As everything is happening so fast it is hard to get the help we need as there simply isn't enough staff. The hospice nurse offers to call Needs Assessment & Service Co-ordination for help is necessary. They will apply for help three times a day through the home care agency and tell them it's urgent. I am told I might be able to get night-time help through a private home care agency or through the hospice. It all

sounds very confusing. I don't care how much it will cost or how it is done as long as something is done! I am at my wits' end and completely exhausted.

10 am: My uncle from overseas arrives, accompanied by an aunt. He is visibly shocked and holds Mum's hand. They are able to talk a little. When someone asks what time it is, Mum checks her watch. We think it's kind of funny because she still wants to be in control but for her it means that she *is* in control.

10.50 am: I give Mum all her medication, followed by breakfast. She can take very small amounts of water and soft food only which I give to her in quantities of drops on a teaspoon. She is able to sit slightly raised in bed. I also gave her extra pain relief. 'I fed her like a baby bird', I think.
"Like a sparrow," she says.

3.30 pm: I give Mum her meds and 'lunch' - just a tiny bit of banana cake. She has more trouble swallowing pills now.

About 3.40 pm: We get a visitor, a devotee friend who asks Mum if she would like to listen to some music.
"Shall I put the Gayatri mantra on?" I ask.
I get the CD player from the dining room and plug it in under the window near the bed end and play the mantra softly on a continuous loop. It is very soothing for her as well as myself. Also visitors saying their last goodbyes comment on it. We listen to it ever since.

When the hospice nurse comes later in the afternoon, she helps me change my mum's sanitary pad. She asks me to get a nightie, and tells me to cut it in half all the way along the back. She explains that this way it will be much easier for my mum be cared for as we won't need to lift my mum up to put her head and arms through her nightie. The reality hits me hard. There is no turning back now. I can hardly get it over my heart to cut her nightie and I distract myself with some other things for a while before I can get myself to do it. I find a comfortable light blue soft flannelette nightgown with tiny little white flowers. I don't want to do it but I know I have to. I take a deep breath and when I cut the gown I can feel tears flowing over my cheeks. The nurse is very patient and gentle for which I am very grateful. She manages to keep herself busy until I am ready. She then teaches me how to administer morphine through a thin, plastic tube which she has inserted

The Father
The Son
The Holy Spirit
there's no turning
back

into my mum's right upper arm. I will have to screw off the end of the syringe containing the morphine before injecting it into the line. 'Blue end', I write down. I give her either one or half a mil of morphine, as needed. I am given a plastic bag with six syringes containing morphine, and another one with six syringes containing a saline solution to clear the line afterwards. I will need to keep them in the fridge. In a booklet given by the nurse I have to record the dose each time I administer it, and write down the hospice community support phone number in case I need help.

After an emotional, almost telepathic exchange Mum points at her left hand. She is trying to reach the silver ring with a red garnet on her middle finger. It is quite a gesture, no words are spoken. I don't know quite what to say. She makes it clear to me that she wants me to remove it from her finger. I put some lotion around her finger so that the ring can slide off easily.

5.06 pm: My mum has gone into a deep sleep. I take a few photographs. She looks so relaxed and beautiful. Her head rests on top of a small light blue towel, covering her pillow. Her mouth is slightly open and right hand lies relaxed up on her shoulder. She will be ready to leave soon.

About 5.50 pm: I insert a line in the right arm for pain relief and agitation/nausea.

I know that I will need to say goodbye to my mother soon, and mentally make a note that I need to ring the doctor at the medical centre to ask for a copy of the oncologist's notes as it might help me with writing my eulogy. I know it's not inappropriate, yet it feels weird and I almost feel apologetic for it.

About 6.40 pm: Mum has gone into a deep relaxed state, breathing deeply with some longer pauses in between.

About 11 pm: The night-time carer arrives and will stay until 7.30 am so that I can take some much needed rest. She will call me if anything changes. I help her change Mum into a nightie. She's rather clumsy and the line comes out of her arm. I ring the hospice 24-hour number who advise me that it's OK for now. They tell me that a hospice nurse will come tomorrow and put in a new line and that I will be able to give Mum her meds as usual by giving it to her crushed between two spoons, mixed with yoghurt.

Day 12

5.28 am: Mum needs extra pain relief. I give it to her crushed in yoghurt, followed by some more yoghurt with some honey mixed into it.

6.05 am: I give her an enema (it's the last one in the box, I see). Remembering that yesterday morning she had a glance at the pictures of my late brother again I wonder if she thought she might be seeing him in the afterlife.

9.25 am: I give her half a dose of the first morphine injection through the new line inserted by the hospice nurse.

9.40 am: For breakfast I give Mum yoghurt with honey, banana and pineapple juice.

At some point during the morning she beckons me from her bed and says weakly: "I want to show you the saris."
I am very relieved and grateful because I have been waiting for this moment. I know there is not much time left and she can barely bring up the energy to speak now. Her wardrobe is on an angle opposite her bed so she is unable to see inside of it. I open the wardrobe door and one by one I show her each sari of the colours she described when I first arrived.
"Is it this one?" I start. "This one? This one?" Only choosing from the golds and blues in her large collection.
She examines each one carefully and finally says: "Yes, that one. Put that in your wardrobe."
I do as she says so that I will have the right one on the actual day. The sari is beautiful. It is golden yellow silk fabric of about six metres long with tiny turquoise and red shiny dots glittering along one side of it. This one is to be placed over the casket.
I show her some more, until she says: "Yes, that one."

The outfit consists of loose punjabi pants, a tunic and a scarf made of royal blue silk with gold embroidery. This is the one she will be wearing inside the coffin. I will need to ask one of my mum's devotee friends to help me with her dressing for the viewing, as on my own I wouldn't know how to drape the garment correctly or appropriately for the occasion.

About 11.25 am: I give Mum her second morphine injection, half a dose.

12.30 pm: I feed Mum one pineapple piece to suck on after which she spits out the fibre. She drinks a quarter cup of water.

1.30 pm: The social worker arrives. He is very friendly and easy to get along with. He already knows my mum from her time working as a volunteer.

I have written down some questions that I still need answered, such as whether she wants Jesus or Mary mentioned at her funeral service as she was raised as a Catholic, considering she is so heavily involved with the Sai Baba group. I also hope that she can be more specific with regard to spreading her ashes, and not just the general 'on the land'. And where can I find the will?

I ask the social worker if he will be so kind as to take notes for me when I ask her those questions as it has become very hard to understand every word she says because of her weakness. She has started to mumble a lot more now and I need to look at her intently while we communicate. I want to fulfil her wishes as much as I possibly can and listen closely. I am very grateful that the social worker obliges and I give him my notebook and pen.

He notes: '- Ashes scattered over the land.
       - devotee to talk.
       - the solicitor - will.

                            -> Give back hearing aid domes.
                            -> Call funeral home name.
                            -> Bhajans to be sung
                                  - Gayatri Mantra.

After he gives my notebook back to me, I notice a beautiful Om symbol drawing at the bottom of one of the pages with 'Aum Shanti' written underneath.

In the living room away from my mum, I ask him questions with regard to what I will need to do once Mum has passed away. He tells me that I will need to contact her GP (again I remind myself to get the hospital notes from the oncologist), the hospice, the lawyer, and the funeral home.

5 pm: Morphine 2.5mg given (half a dose).

The hospice nurse arrives again. My mum asks me if I can buy some ice cream.
I ask her: "What kind of ice cream would you like?"
She answers: "What can I have?" Her voice has become a lot weaker now.
"Anything you like," I say lovingly. I almost sound angelic.
"Hokey pokey," she says.
She also asks me to buy a fresh pineapple so that I can make her some fresh pineapple juice. She has been looking forward to that specifically. I know that most likely this will be her last meal - 'The last supper', I think to myself.

I hardly want to leave her side, but the hospice nurse is present so I drive to the supermarket and the veggie shop. I drive with tears rolling down my face and need to gather myself before getting out of the car. When I return I stir some ice cream in a suitable little bowl until it is completely soft. I am able to feed it to her from a teaspoon, a drop at a time. She can barely close her mouth but she waits for me with her mouth open like a hungry baby bird, fed by its mother. She seems to enjoy it very much.

5.49 pm: My mum is asleep and looks very peaceful and relaxed with her mouth open and both hands up, the same way babies often sleep. Both the necklaces are lying on her chest. I feel I need to take a photo of her.

I have lots of mixed feelings. Observing my mother it feels like I am in labour, about to give birth and we're nearly there. We have spoken about death a lot. Mum says: "You are born with a cry and you go out with a smile and that's what I'm doing." She's a free spirit, always has been and soon she will fly free. No longer will she have to be tired or be in pain. Others are waiting for her in the spirit world, she has told me. She says: "Angels cry when you are born and the people are so happy. But when you die the people are sad and the angels are so happy to have you back."

I start to draw lots of little hearts now, in my notebook. 'This is Mum's eighty-fourth year ♡', I write.

I remember looking at a photograph of Mum when she was pregnant with me, doing something with my bassinet. At first glance she looked like an absolute goddess. I tell her that, just after feeding her a few mouse bites of apricot custard. I thought she had gone into some kind of sleep state but she must have heard me because she says: "I *am* a goddess." ♡

I tell her I am so happy to have had her as my mum.
She answers: "Because I wanted you."
When I tell her I will miss her, she says: "Don't cry meisje (girl), it's only the body."

I am so privileged to be able to be by my mum's side and guide her through the beautiful and amazing process of dying.
She says: "It's a blessing for me and a blessing for you."
It appears very much like she is in labour of herself, about to give birth to herself on the other side. The Gayatri mantra is helping us both in the process and provides much peace and support. I feel deep sadness and at the same time I am happy because soon she will be free.

7.34 pm: "Can you pass me my walking stick?" she asks.
"Your walking stick???" I say.
"To go to the toilet," she says.
"It's OK to go in your nappy," I say, carefully.
She looks determined. The walking stick leans in the corner against the wall and the wardrobe just behind me. It's a lightweight retractable metal stick, white with pink and purple flowers and little green leaves. It has a gold rim between the stick and the black plastic handle. "I bought this at the pharmacy, nice isn't it?" I remember her saying about a week ago. I put the handle of her walking stick into her hand as she doesn't really open her eyes anymore. She works really hard with a determined frown on her face, moving the stick, tapping it around against the

mattress and the rail of the bed. I feel helpless but I have to let her. After a few minutes she relaxes and I ask if she is finished. I wait a moment.

"Can I have it now?" I ask gently. I take the stick out of her hand and place it back against the wall.

8.06 pm: I give her morphine, 2.5mg as she indicates pain in the groin.

8.22 pm: Mum tells me she might pass over any minute.

"Why is that?" I ask.

She replies: "I can hear the angels calling."

I hold her hand. I tell her I'm so happy for her that she can be a free spirit again.

8.26 pm: I have been fanning her face since she has been too weak to do it herself for a few days now, so when she asks for her fan I start fanning her face. She looks annoyed and moves her hand, impatiently gesturing that she wants to do it herself. I place the plastic handle of the paper fan into her hand and she starts fanning her own face. She can only just do it, with her arm and hand up, supported by her pillow. She waves the fan a little beside her face, just above the pillow. Her eyes are closed and her mouth is open. Her left hand is resting on her left shoulder. I give her healing ♡ while she is holding her fan. I admire that in her state of helplessness she is still so determined to remain independent.

8.50 pm: I read her my poem in the second person:

"You are a Light Being

At the Speed of Light

you travel on your Light Beam

through Time Infinite

and Beyond

Light is where you left

and Light is where you're going

while in the meanTime

on your LightWay

you Light Up

All There Is

with your Eyes

your Hands

your Voice
your Heart
You Radiate
and Penetrate
the Positive,
the Negative
(as One they Live)
You Shine
and
All your Love
you Give",

immediately followed by another reading in the first person:

"I'm a Light Being
At the Speed of Light
I travel on my Light Beam
through Time Infinite
and Beyond
Light is where I left
and Light is where I'm going
while in the meanTime
on my LightWay
I Light Up
All There Is
with my Eyes
my Hands
my Voice
my Heart
I Radiate
and Penetrate
the Positive,
the Negative
(as One they Live)
I Shine
and
All my Love

I Give."

'The sweetest human being on the planet and in the world ♡', I write.

9 pm: Mum asks for a bowl of water to wash her hands. I know it can't be long to go now. I understand that the water signifies purification. In the kitchen I find a suitable white ceramic bowl, not too large, not too small, and fill it half full with purified water. From the bathroom I get a large and soft light blue towel, fold it lengthwise and drape it across her body in case of spillage. I place the bowl on the towel on the bed, first on her right, then on her left side and lift her hands, one at a time to help her find the bowl. I help her dip her fingers in the water. She is very conscious of her actions. I know she is ready to go now. Once I have taken the bowl off the bed I place it on the floor and dry her hands. I am thankful no water has overflowed the brim of the bowl.

9.09 pm: She asks if the tip of her nose is white.
"No, why?" I ask. I feel like I am lying a little as I did notice the bottom triangle of her nose around the nostrils look white, even in the darkness of the room I could see it.
"Because then I'm dead," she replies.
"You're still breathing," I tell her.
The whole notion is so interesting. Did she think she was dead? Is her transition from life into death lifting the veil, obscuring reality? By the sound of it my mother didn't know where she was, in that moment. More like a floating in vacant space. 'Is this proof there is consciousness after death?' I think.

9.11 pm: She asks for pineapple juice. I spoon some drops onto her lips so that the fluid can run into her mouth. I have mixed the juice with a bit of honey to sweeten the slightly overripe pineapple. She can now no longer close her mouth and can hardly swallow. I am careful to make sure not too much liquid falls off the spoon so that she won't choke.

9.16 pm: Mum wants the fan again. I fan her face.

9.25 pm: I give her a few drops of ice cream.

9.46 pm: Mum indicates she has a sore groin and I administer 2.5mg of morphine through the line in her arm. I start to fan her whole body now.

10.10 pm: She asks me: "Am I still breathing?"
"Yes," I say, "you're still breathing, we are still talking."
As if she doesn't quite believe me, she lifts her right hand towards her face and touches her face all over with her finger tips, checking to see if she is still alive.

10.14 pm: I feed her some very soft ice cream off a teaspoon.
"Yum," she says, clearly.
Some more drops of ice cream, then some pineapple juice.

10.59 pm: She wants more cold ice cream so I feed her some more drops off the spoon.

11.09 pm: I give her some drops of pineapple juice.

11.17 pm: I administer morphine 2.5mg by injection through the line in her arm as she shows me pain in the groin.

"Everyone is waiting," she says. "Two brothers, uncles, aunts, and the dog," referring to the little white poodle we used to have a long time ago.
'No mention of my grandparents, my brother or my father though', I think to myself.

Day 13

00.10 am: I need to lie down and close my eyes for some time while the caregiver stays with mum ♡ This is the second night we have the privilege of a caregiver.

4.23 am: I try to resist but have to throw up loudly and feel much better afterwards.

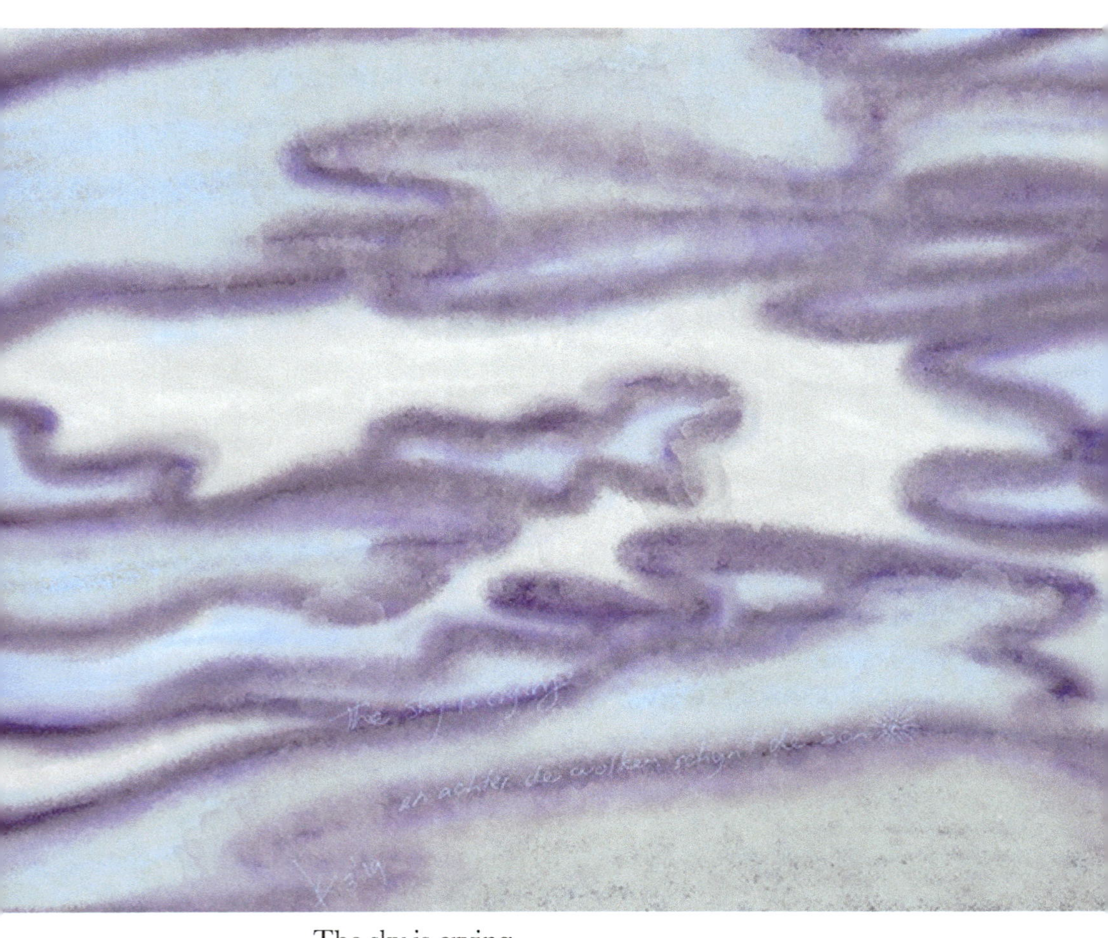

The sky is crying
en achter de wolken schijnt the zon ☀

In my notebook I write: 'May your spirit live on through my words ♡'. I hope I will be able to do her justice.

During the night my mum mumbles something, a memory from a time long before I was born, about her old employer: "She always said," she starts, and continues: "You may be praying to Petrus, but…"
I know she is referring to St Peter, the guardian of the Heavenly Gates. She then continues with some babble I cannot understand no matter how hard I listen. I know she is saying something comical because I have heard this story before and I am happy to hear that even now she still shows her sense of humour.
She continues: "…but then you can you can shit it out again too!! - Piet - Petronella (one of her names) - Petrus," she adds - as if that explains everything.

About 7 am: Mum appears to have been fully asleep since around midnight. When I tell the night carer this she tells us: "I'm not sleeping, I was dozing."

About 7.10 am: She tries to pull her mala and silver necklace down, away from her throat. I help her get them out and pull them onto her chest.

7.17 am: Mum indicates she needs more pain relief by pulling a knee up, and I can see it by her facial expression. I ask if she wants more pain relief.
She nods and makes a confirming sound: "Mmm".
I administer morphine, 2.5mg.

Just before 8 am: I comb her hair. She will appreciate that because my eighty-nine-year-old uncle will be visiting again, one more time before he leaves the country. When he arrives he is visibly shocked to see his sister lying there and how fast she is waning. She is so weak. Nothing is said but the emotions are running high. My uncle just holds Mum's hand. I leave them alone.

10.44 am: I give her more morphine, another dose of 2.5mg.

The deep sleeping and deep breathing continues during the day. More visitors come to say their last goodbyes. My mum senses a close friend in the room and turns her head towards him. Her eyes open suddenly and she looks straight at him. I can see her eyes wide open and they look very glassy. I have not seen them like that before and I don't know if she can actually see him. I can't help feeling ever so slightly jealous as she looks directly at him but I know how important this is for them both. I can see he is choked up so I get up and leave them be for a while.

I feel her fingers around my hand. When I tell her I love her she responds reassuringly by stretching her fingers out over my wrist. ♡

The breathing is getting louder now and there are some short pauses in between. Mum has not moved her left arm or hand all night or day. Just the right hand she moves occasionally up to her face or tummy.

'May your spirit be carried on through the words I speak ♡', I write.

6.25 pm-ish: Very deep breathing is starting now.

7.04 pm: Heavy breathing, some longer pauses at times and she makes some sounds.

8.33 pm: Like a marathon to the Seventh Heaven. It's almost like giving birth, but this time to herself ♡ It's not easy for her. She's working hard, as if she is running uphill or up the stairs, towards the light. Previously she had described to me a beautiful golden light and I can almost see the light for myself. It is heavenly and she can't get there fast enough. It's a long road, uphill. I can feel the emotion running through her body and I perceive facial expressions indicating jubilant excitement. I can hear her silent crying out for deliverance. This must be heaven for sure. It's as if I can hear the heavenly singing of the angels with my own ears and I am so happy for my mum that the end of the road here, is near.

8.44 pm: I give her morphine for pain in the groin, which she indicates with her right hand and voice.

About 9.40 pm: There is much and constant rattling going on. I am super exhausted and can hardly keep my eyes open. But I do not want to leave my mother's side. I need to stay awake, at any cost. I am really struggling; I have really run out of energy. Just like my mum seems to be in labour, I feel like I am in the process of giving birth to myself, too. A few months later the words 'the death of you, is the death of me', come to my mind. As if I too, am emerging from my old skin.

I am not sure what to do at this point. I know we are getting so close now. Shall I hold her hand? Mum has not moved for a while now, and both arms are lying next to her side. I try to slide my hand under hers. It is not as easy as I thought as she doesn't seem to cooperate. Her fingers are not as relaxed as I imagined they would be. I manage to get my hand into hers and hold it. I am full of anticipation and I don't even know why or for what. I have never been in this situation before. I want to be here, for my mum. I want her to know that I am here and that I am supporting her for as long as I can. It is hot and apparently annoyed she suddenly pulls her hand out of mine. 'She wants to leave', I think. But I still put my hand back into hers. I am not ready to give her up yet. I ponder and consider the possibility that our physical contact will hinder her from slipping away into death. 'She is well on her way', I think. I let her go and tell her that I love her.

I am at a bit of a loss. Is there anything that needs to be said still, before it's too late? I think back over the years gone by. I recall our complicated, almost love/hate relationship. I tell her that if we ever see each other again in a different life, I hope that we will be a whole lot better at relationships because we sure were not good at it this time around. Given the recent responses I am relatively sure that she can hear me. "I will miss you so much," I say through my tears.

10.45 pm: The caregiver arrives. A different girl this time, very sweet and capable and we have an instant connection. I still stay up with her for about an hour. We quietly sit by Mum's side in the dark room.

11.49 pm: More deep breathing. Mum's breathing has really sped up during the day.

Day 14

1.08 am: I am woken up by the loud and fast breathing of my mum in her room across the hallway. I am alarmed. This sounds much louder and faster than before.

As if she is running now, panting hard. I know this must be *it*. I rush up to be by her side. The caregiver tells me that she is in the last cycle of breathing which started about midnight just after I went to bed.

1.52 am: Even faster breathing and panting now and she's gurgling a bit, almost as if running to the top of the hill. Her expression seems lit with euphoria and surprise as if in seventh heaven, and even with sadness. Such a contrast to her feelings of misery over the last few weeks.

1.55 am: My mother has passed her last breath ♡. She just stopped. I stare in disbelief. I turn around and look at the caregiver. I see that she is crying silently.
"Is this it?" I ask.
She nods. "Yes, this is it," she says and apologises for her tears. "It gets me every time," she says.

'I love you Mum ♡', I write in my notebook. She looks so peaceful.

It has been quick, but not easy.

Life is a perpetual cycle of births and deaths. When one door closes, another one opens. I contemplate the meaning of death and the meaning of birth, metaphorically speaking. We give birth to ourselves when we are born, then again as women we give birth to another being. And when we do, again, we give birth to ourselves as a mother. So, when we die in one life, we may be born in another.

When leaving our body we enter another realm. I truly believe my mother when she said that angels, people and animals who went before us are waiting with open arms. ♡

"She has won the marathon," I say to the caregiver.

♡

As Mum said: "We are born on the other side."

♡

   'May you live
         forth forever.
In my heart forever ♡', I write in my notebook.

And in my diary I write: '♡ This morning 1.55 am Mum ♡
♡ passed her last breath ♡
♡ peacefully at home ♡
♡ I love you Mum ♡'

2.46 am: As I feel her face
her chest
I know the body is cooling down.
I still perceive movement
up and down
in the chest
as if breathing
as if asleep.

About 3 am: I put the blue blanket over her ♡ to make her look comfortable, as if asleep.

4 am: I am checking in on Mum. The colour has now completely gone from her face.
'Time to ring the hospice soon', I note.

4.44 am: '♡ Thank you for waiting ♡
♡ for me when passing ♡
♡ That was the greatest gift! ♡

I will have a rest now ♡', I write.

PART 3

Down to Earth

I notice that over the course of the night Mum's facial expression has changed. She is now completely relaxed. From ecstasy to sadness and peace, I can almost compare it to watching a newborn baby's face changing its expression many times. It is just so curious. Her mouth was wide open while she took her last breath but as I check on her from time to time I see that her mouth has closed much more during the night, until just slightly open, in the morning.

Early in the morning I sit down with the caregiver. She is very lovely and we talk about the night. She tells me that my mum was so relieved when I walked into her room at 1.08 am.

"She looked very worried," she says. "But as soon as you walked through the door her face relaxed. I think she was worried that you weren't going to make it," she says.

I ask her what to do next. She suggests that I ring the doctor soon, and the funeral home. She has noticed the photo album from India. We go through the album together and she is in awe.

"Is your mum's funeral going to be like this?" she asks.

I tell her that my mum has told me what she wants to wear at her funeral and that she has wanted me to ask for a speaker from her spiritual group. She asks if she can come to the funeral.

"Of course," I say. I promise I will send her an invitation. Once the caregiver is gone I comb my mum's hair to make her look beautiful.

9 am: The doctor arrives to confirm the death. It's the first time I meet him and I can see why my mother liked him. In a way he reminds me of our old GP back in our home country. He examines her in private. I tell him that my mum had told me how much she liked him. At last I ask him if it will be OK for him to send me the hospital notes with regard to my mum's occupation. He kindly agrees.

10.30 am: My mum looks so peaceful and even seems to smile a little now. She really has arrived at her destination. She is so beautiful. The funeral directors arrive, a man and a woman. They are very pleasant to deal with and very down to earth, something I really like about them. They are very matter of fact and don't beat around the bush either. When I take them to see my mum they ask me how old she is and are very surprised.
"Eighty-three? Her skin looks amazing! She looks very young for her age!" they exclaim.
Well of course she *is* very relaxed, now.

As long as I can remember Mum has always looked much younger than her actual age. She seems to have remained timeless over the years. I tell them that I would like to be involved in the process and that I would like to help them put my mum onto the trolley that they have brought. They are happy for me to help and park the trolley parallel to the bed.

I take the brakes off the hospital bed so I can slide myself in between the bed and the wall, in my mother's very small room. We decide to keep Mum's jewellery on until the cremation when the pieces can be removed. We count two silver rings, two necklaces and one watch. More than eight hours have passed since she died. Rigor mortis has set in fully. Her body is completely stiff now. Without being disrespectful it reminds me of a stuffed possum. Everything happens so fast and I see that they have rolled her onto her left side facing myself and the wall. As I stand behind the bed I am asked to support my mum's shoulder and hip to keep her stable while they tuck a rolled-up white sheet underneath her body. It's all very matter of fact now and I hear my mother's voice say: "It's just the body", which is exactly how I perceive it too. I don't feel my mother's presence within the body - it is just the body.

As my mum is rolled over I am horrified at the strong, unpleasant odour once the bottom sheet and sanitary pad are exposed to the air. I can see now that there has been leakage and there is a brownish stain on the sheet. I feel for her. I know that my mum's body had begun to shut down days ago. But the reality of it all hits me in the face. There is no denial now.

The funeral directors skilfully and swiftly manoeuvre the white sheet underneath my mum's body so that they can transfer it onto the trolley. Her whole body is wrapped in the sheet which is crossed over beautifully with just her face sticking out. Two black straps are tied crosswise over her chest and another around her legs. The black straps make it look as if she has her arms crossed across the chest and to me she looks like an Egyptian goddess. She looks so beautiful, graceful and peaceful. I carefully kiss her on her forehead. One of the funeral directors shows me a large rectangular, clear, hard plastic sheet.
"Do you mind if we put this over her face?" he asks. "Just so we can protect her face," he adds.
I nod. I leave the room so that they can do their work. I wait in the guest bedroom across the narrow hallway from my mum's room.

They are ready now to roll her out of her room and into the hallway, out of the house. A dark blue velvet cloth covers her entire body now.
"We can't get her out of the room," the man says.
I know the corner is tight and narrow.
Both look at me apologetically and say: "We will have to put her up I'm sorry."
I say that it's OK, I have seen this before. I remember watching a dead neighbour being carried out through the front door of his house vertically on a stretcher, before they could put him in the ambulance. I was about six and very fascinated with the event.

They are now able to get my mum out of her room and back onto the trolley in the hallway. The trolley wheels leave deep marks on the parquet floor as they roll it towards the lounge. Once they are there my mother is covered with a turquoisey-green quilt with a decorative motif, draped across the body so that it overhangs the trolley. Then, the trolley is pushed outside through the sliding doors onto the wooden deck, up towards the street where their station wagon is parked. I follow them outside with a heavy heart and watch them slide the collapsed trolley into the back of their station wagon. I watch them drive off and down the street until I can no longer see them. Tears are streaming down my face. 'This is it, then', I think. I walk back towards the house.

As soon as I enter the living room I am amazed by the huge tangible weight lifting off my shoulders. I am so relieved and at the same time I feel empty and drained. My head spins from all the activity. There is still a lot to do.

1.45 pm: Another member of the funeral home arrives to talk about the details of the funeral. I am grateful that I have been able to discuss this with my mum. Not long after my arrival she told me that she was thinking of having a viewing in the living room - on the coffee table maybe. I was very doubtful about that idea but I didn't tell her that I found it a bit creepy. It wouldn't be very practical either considering the small space and the potential number of people coming. She had told me that she didn't want to be embalmed. I knew what she wanted to wear and that she wanted a simple, cheap coffin. "A cardboard coffin is all I need," she had said, "with a golden sari over it." She wanted to be cremated.

As we discuss the details the funeral director tells me that we cannot have a viewing if the body is not embalmed. I insist that we do a viewing as that is what my mum wanted.
"I am simply trying to do everything according to my mother's wishes," I say.
After a short telephone discussion with colleagues she suggests to have the viewing at a chapel, a different venue where the body can be kept cool. She has been told that the body is 'in very bad condition'. Decay of the body must be evident.

She tells me that a viewing will be possible, but for strictly one hour only. I concede. As no embalming will be allowed, she asks for permission to drain the body of excess fluid so that no fluids can escape from the body. She explains that the tumours will still continue to grow for a while and the body will keep bloating. She also asks that Mum's eyes and mouth will be treated so that they will not open while we dress her, or during the viewing. 'That would completely freak people out', I think, so I agree as technically this is not part of the embalming process and makes perfect sense. The viewing will be held as soon as possible the following day. The funeral itself will take place in our local town three or four days after that, whichever suits best.

There is a long list of things which need to be done. I have to notify family, neighbours, friends. I need to get a death certificate for the solicitor, insurance company, the bank, and other service providers. I will be expecting about one hundred people.

We agree to have the viewing at 1pm so I will have to get there myself at 12pm so we will have an hour to get my mum dressed. I make a note to bring the mala and put it in my bag so I won't forget. I say that I will take care of the service sheet myself as I have the skills to do that. We have a look through some service sheet samples and I take some photographs of them to get an idea of how I want my mum's to look. I go for an A5 size folded card and decide to have my poem on the inside. I need to contact the speaker who will lead the service and inform him with regard to the timing of everything so that he can plan his speech. My mum wanted bhajans to be sung. The funeral director suggests it will be a good idea to 'sing her out', while she is carried from the chapel to the hearse.

I decide to have the funeral four days after the viewing which will give me time to design and create the service sheet and contact everyone. The service sheet is due at the funeral home two days before the funeral at 4 pm. It is to be sent as a PDF file, as a double-sided A4. The newspaper notice is due on the day after the viewing. The funeral director suggests that I buy a memorial book for people to sign, and buy red petals to put on the casket. She suggests cream Columbia roses or gerberas which are popular at the moment for a floral tribute. I feel no connection with those flowers whatsoever so I decide to check out the florist for myself. My mum had said no flowers but I think it will be appropriate to put up at least something small. The funeral director tells me the address of a local florist and suggests I go there this afternoon to see what kind of pieces they can do for me. When I drive down to see them I have a look at the selection available and look through some books. Still, nothing really stands out.

From the time of my mum's passing I can feel her strong presence with me like a sheet of electricity prickling my entire back, specifically when I have to make important decisions or just when she lets me know that she 'has my back', supporting my resolve. About four days after mum's passing I can feel her like a warm blanket wrapping me from behind. She is still with me, I know, and I find comfort in that.

We talk about putting a bereavement notice in the paper, and live streaming the funeral service. Who will the speakers be from the family? I make note to check mum's contacts as some of them may want to say a few words. For the death certificate I need my grandparents' full names - in the correct spelling. I note that I still need to get hold of mum's occupation notes from the oncologist, even though I do know her life story.

Finally, I turn off the CD player.

Day 15

10 am: Early in the morning I suddenly get some inspiration. I can see cream tulips and roses clearly now. They actually mean something to me and my mum. Tulips for the country connection and roses for the roses my mum has loved growing in her gardens. Before my mother's dressing and viewing I drive to the florist to see what they can do for a flower arrangement. Just before leaving I realise I have not yet thought about footwear to match mum's outfit. In a shoe cupboard in the garage I find beautiful velvet flats. They look brand new and are the exact same colour as the punjabi my mum will be wearing: royal blue. There are bows on top with gold details at the end of the laces. They are perfect.

At the florist the second time round I know the roses and tulips are the right decision. I can clearly feel my mum's electricity tingle, all over my back. I ask that they arrange a flat kind of piece in the shape of a fanlike peacock's tail, and not too big. I think it will look nice placed in front of the casket. In Hindu religion peacocks are used as a symbol of the cycle of time and is also associated with the goddess Saraswati, a deity representing benevolence, patience, kindness, compassion and knowledge. In Christianity too, the peacock is a symbol of eternal life and represents the "all-seeing" church, along with the holiness and sanctity associated with it. In addition the peacock represents resurrection, renewal and immortality. (Source: *Sanskriti Magazine*, https://m.dailyhunt.in/news.)

The florist is not quite sure how create such a piece as she has never done anything like it and there's nothing in her sample books she can compare it to.
"Just be creative," I tell her with a smile. I trust that she will come up with something beautiful.

Just after 12 pm: I arrive at the funeral chapel. In a back room the funeral director and one of mum's devotee friends are waiting for me so we can dress my mother together. When I first walk into the room through the back entrance behind the chapel I can see my mother lying on top of a pink sheet draped over a trolley. At the head end there's a small pillow underneath the sheet so that my mum's head is elevated. Her body is undressed underneath a white sheet, folded at the top so that it looks like she's asleep. I can see by the silhouette she is wearing an adult nappy and that her tummy is a bit bloated. Still, she looks dignified, like a queen. Along the wall there is a wooden chair with cream cushioning on the back and seat. Next to the chair a side table with a glowing salt lamp, a box of tissues, turquoise green and blue silicon gloves, and a vase with one rose. I put my shoulder bag in the corner of the room, on the floor. I realise how special this time is with my mum - another one in a lifetime experience. At first glance I can see that the muscles around her mouth look slightly unnatural and almost give her a staunch look like 'I am doing this'. Her chin looks a bit higher than usual, determined not to drop and her lips are telling me the same thing. She looks happy though, her eyes are shut and she looks proud, waiting patiently.

Dressing mum's body is a challenge. By now her body has become completely limp, like a rag doll. I kiss her on the forehead. I can't get over how *cold* she is. Mum's friend and the funeral director wear a white plastic apron and latex gloves. I am glad mum's friend is there because I wouldn't know how the punjabi goes together. The outfit is made of very thin silk and consists out of wide pants, a short sleeved tunic and a scarf. The tunic has at least two thin layers of fabric. The silk fabric is not stretchy so we have to work as a team to get my mum dressed. The pants go on first. To get the tunic over mum's head I lift her head and support her upper back while mum's friend guides her head through the opening. Then the arms, one at a time. The arm holes are rather tight and we have to pull the arms up high to get them through the sleeves. We feel rather chuffed with ourselves, except that the inner lining of the tunic stays above mum's chest and is all bunched up. I try to carefully pull it down but we soon figure out that the stroppy silk needs a bit more encouragement so I really start tugging it down, underneath the top layer. The treatment is rather rough but it's the only way.
"I bet my mum is laughing now," I say. "She always used to say if you want to be beautiful, you will have to suffer", I explain, apologetically.
Suddenly I notice a lot of flakey powder on the tunic. It really stands out against the blue. The funeral director sees it too.

"That's dead skin cells," she clarifies.
It's a little macabre but she has probably seen it hundreds of times.

The friend's husband arrives. It's good timing because we are ready to transfer the body into the casket which has been brought in by the funeral director. The casket is a simple plywood box with cream satin lining on the inside. Three silver handles for the pallbearers on each side. The funeral director describes the best way to do the transfer. I will support my mother's head. The others space themselves evenly along the body so we all support her weight. We are able to put Mum's body into the casket in one fluid move. Mum's friend drapes the long scarf around her neck, down the front and rubs some vibhuti on her forehead. My mum is still wearing her watch and her jewellery: a crystal mala with yellow gold tassel and a silver necklace with a silver Om pendant around her neck, and her rings. In her right hand we place the wooden mala she used to hold on to in bed and later had this lying under her pillow. A devotee has given a little bag of vibhuti to go with Mum. We put this under the scarf. It all looks very natural now. We don't apply any make-up. At last we reposition the little pillow underneath her head so it doesn't tilt forward. I comb her hair. She looks so peaceful and beautiful. But more importantly, she looks contented. Later another packet of materialised vibhuti is given which we tuck underneath the scarf on the other side. This is exactly how she would have wanted it.

We finish just before the commencement of the viewing so it's perfect timing. We roll her from the back room through the chiller area and then through a heavy curtain into the chapel. The casket sits on a small trolley covered with a sage green cloth. We position it underneath some spotlights. The lights shine beautifully on Mum's face. She is just glowing.

Inside the chapel already a number of people are seated. I quickly give the CD with the Gayatri mantra to the funeral director who plays it softly in the background. A lot of people, most of them devotees, take the opportunity to bid Mum farewell. I call them her 'Sai family'. One of the ladies brings a poem she channelled earlier in the morning. I take a photograph of it and place it next to her in the casket. Other friends bring flowers: I see beautiful bright colours in geraniums and lots of roses. They put them in the casket with my mum. She looks even more beautiful now.

Time to shine!

After the viewing we have a brief discussion about the actual funeral service in a few days time. Someone suggests putting a framed photograph on top of the casket. I disagree because in my opinion everyone has their own memories of my mum and they should remember her as they knew her.

The next few days

The next few days are crazy busy as well. I need to organise the venue for refreshments after the service. It takes a few trips to potential places but eventually we decide on the local community centre. I have told the funeral director that I will create the service sheet for the funeral myself. Instantly I know that the photo I took two months ago, will have to be the one on the front of the card. She looks amazing. Full of life, full of love… 'Who would have thought her life on earth would end so soon?' I think. Looking at it it's almost as if she asks: "Is it good? Do you think it's OK?" when reading out her little SOS paper. She also looks brave and even encouraging, as if to say: "Go on, you can do it."

Next to her on the couch you can see a cream-coloured cushion which she made for me a few years ago. It has red and green embroidered poppies on it. It is as solid as a rock but it looks very pretty so I have always cherished it.

I find a suitable font for the card and write at the top: 'In Loving Memory'. At the bottom her name, date of birth and date of death. Inside the card for the background I choose a photograph which I took on the beach a few days earlier. The same beach my mum used to walk on most days, when she still could. On the left page I write: 'A celebration of the life of' followed by the address of the service and thank the speaker and the funeral director. Then the order of service with the name of the person leading the service, myself with a eulogy and poem, other tributes, bhajans, and farewell. At the bottom of the page an invitation for all to share their memories and enjoy light refreshments at the conclusion of the service. On the right-hand side I write my poem with above it a flying dove, looking down at the poem and the beach. It took me exactly twenty-one shots of the little dove she had sitting on top of her bathroom mirror to capture the perfect image for this.

On the back of the card I insert a photograph of my mother in India. She is wearing a burgundy and gold sari with a little embroidered fabric bag hanging across her shoulders. But most of all she is wearing a big happy smile. I can just see some toes sticking out from under the sari. Underneath I write: 'She who is'. At the bottom I place the Om symbol which I have photographed from an embroidered tablecloth Mum had draped over her little altar.

Next to Mum's photograph I write the Gayatri mantra, which has been so soothing all through the process:

Om Bhur Bhuvah Swah
Tat-savitur Varenyam
Bhargo Devasya Dhimahi
Dhiyo Yonar Prachodayat

Underneath I insert an English interpretation from a Sai website:

We meditate on that most
adored Supreme Lord, the
creator, whose effulgence
(divine light) illumines all
realms (physical, mental and
spiritual). May this divine
light illumine our intellect.

It's a beautiful prayer. Underneath it I place a photograph of the pink rose which grew in a pot on my mum's deck. It opened the day Mum died.

Day 18

Tonight I finally have the chance to write my eulogy. I never used the oncologist's notes.

Day 19

Today Mum's funeral is held at the local funeral chapel. When I get there the funeral director has already rolled the casket inside and has taken care to position it in the centre. The casket itself sits on a small trolley covered with black velvet overhanging the sides. Two cream candles are burning. They stand in a glass each on top of two pillars in the corners of diagonal, lavender-coloured walls on either side of the casket. The creamy white centre wall has a TV screen mounted on it. I made the decision not to make use of it just so that each individual can have their own memories running freely through their mind. Together with the funeral director I drape Mum's golden sari over the casket so that it looks even and level from the viewer's perspective.

The floral tribute is stunning and really crowns my mum's last resting place. It is made of cream tulips, roses and gypsum with green ferns and other foliage. It looks like a cross between a peacock's tail and a posy. I know that the size, simplicity and elegance would have been approved by my mum.

Some of the guests are already present and have donated some floral tributes also. Slowly the chapel fills up with people - friends, family and old colleagues. It's a full house and a lot of them have to stand in the foyer or outside to listen to the service. Mum's night caregiver has come too, with her husband.

We play the Gayatri mantra again, on a loop. The speaker opens the service and then invites me to speak, followed by others who wish to say something. All my children have been able to make it and have made their own arrangements to stay. I am so grateful and proud of them all. My young grandchildren in their pretty dresses are well behaved. They just sit down quietly the whole time and take it all in. I know my mum would have been proud of them too! After the speeches a group of devotees come forward to play devotional music on musical instruments I have never seen before, and sing. I turn towards them to watch and feel my foot swaying up and down to the rhythm of the music. The whole funeral is beautiful - just perfect.

I proudly watch my three sons who make up three of the six pallbearers. While people are leaving to go to the community centre for refreshments, we drive to the crematorium. I sit next to the funeral director in the hearse. I find myself turning around a lot to look at the casket covered with the sari, the floral arrangements and a basket of red rose petals surrounding it. I can see the stream of cars with close family following us. It's a little overcast but every now and then the sun shines a beautiful golden light on the casket. I take several photos during our trip. Just like my mother, I like to document everything and this is no exception.

When we arrive, the hearse stops right in front of the building down a driveway, on a rotating platform. At the push of a button above the windscreen inside the car, the platform turns around and automatically positions the car with the rear facing the large open doors. The cremator is already waiting for us: a tall, balding man with a friendly face and a bit of an English accent. He tells me not to worry if I hear big hissing sounds, as that will just be the machine starting up. We wait for the family to arrive. Slowly they find their way down, walking down the curving driveway. They all stand in line, facing the hearse when the funeral director opens the boot.

Inside the building on a floor covered with what looks like mottled grey vinyl, a rectangular area is marked out by black and yellow tape. I can see two steel trolleys, one behind the other. The one closest to the entrance has blue rollers in between the side bars. On both sides of the steel trolley a white sticker says 'WLL 150Kg'. I can see three massive, steel furnaces from floor to almost ceiling. Helmets with big, clear visors hang on large hooks on the side of one of the furnaces. Behind the first trolley stands the second one in front of the furnaces, without rollers. The space we are in is situated beneath the chapel, where cremation services are held. I have been at this place before to attend other funerals but never knew what happened with the caskets after the service. It all makes sense now.

Inside the chapel located above the cremation area, services are held. Once everyone has left, the casket is lowered into a corridor before being rolled into the large cremation area below ground level. 'So this is where we are', I think.

On the left of the furnaces I can see stacks of empty wooden containers for the purpose of holding people's ashes. They look about thirty centimetres long by about ten centimetres high and fifteen centimetres wide. Next to the wooden containers I see a fire extinguisher and a huge red fan to keep the place cool.

Opposite the furnaces I see five more fire extinguishers on the wall underneath a large window which looks into an office-like space. Through the window I can see a wall clock, a wall planner, a paper tray, a pink and yellow sticky note and some A4's stuck to the window. On the right of the window there is a hand basin with a soap dispenser, a paper towel holder and a first aid kit.

The funeral director places my floral tribute on top of the cars and slides the casket partially out of the hearse under everyone's watchful eye. She asks the pallbearers to come forward to carry the casket over to the waiting trolley. Once the casket is positioned on the trolley, the sari is removed by the funeral director who hands it to me. It doesn't really register with me because everything is happening so fast. I am sure my mum would have been happy to have the sari go with her in the fire.

Without the sari on top I can just see the silver name label on top of the casket through the red petals and a couple of white roses. We all are given the opportunity to place the remaining red rose petals from the basket and say our last goodbyes. In their own private thoughts everyone carefully sprinkles some petals on the lid. Even my two little granddaughters who are lifted up by their parents. It is a dignified and beautiful farewell and everyone seems to be satisfied with how it all unfolds. I have not really felt the presence of my mother in the casket at the funeral service and I don't at the crematorium either. It *is* 'just the body'.

Everyone is now quietly standing outside, their heads in their own world. When I look back inside, the cremator is waiting in front of the second trolley with his hands behind his back, facing us with a solemn look on his face. He really looks like the perfect person to do this kind of work. It's beautiful to see and picture perfect. I can't help but eternalise this moment into a photograph. He apologises as he thinks that he's in the way and starts to move but I ask him to come back to where he was. He kindly obliges and takes his place.

Back at the community centre, I am happy to find out from some locals that my mum has participated in several art exhibitions in the exact same room where we are having our refreshments! It's like everything is completely synchronised and the circle is complete.

Day 24

I call the hospice to arrange a time to drop off the commodity chair I borrowed from them and other items such as the pads and sliding sheets. Somehow I remember to do all the things I need to do. I contact the medical equipment hire place so that they can collect the hospital bed. Everyone is very supportive. At the hospice I get to meet one of the staff, a psychologist who knew Mum well through her volunteer work there. She tells me that she came to the funeral and that it was the best funeral she had ever been to. I fully agree.

PART 4

In Retrospect

There is not a day that goes by that I don't think about my mum, or the time I looked after her. I remember details of her passing vividly, at random times. I still shed tears. I contemplate the transition between life and death, and the way Mum described her experience of it with so much clarity. I was amazed at her constant alertness. She had always been sensitive and sharp as a pin. Nothing would go past her unnoticed.

I was very blessed to have her guide me throughout while confined to her chair and later her bed, and how she was able to teach me practical ways to help her when I had to handle her body physically. And I think about how privileged I was to be able to guide her throughout the process of dying.

I think about the miracle of dying. Because it truly is a miracle, just as the birth of a baby is a miracle and it will never cease to amaze me. I think about the notion of the mind agreeing with spirit that the body has to go. I think about dying as a choice, sometimes by will, sometimes by circumstance. And I think about the way people die. I do not believe that my mother ever expected to suffer as much as she did, and neither did I.

I am not trying to sanctify her. I know I have needed to step up to the plate and do everything in my power to make peace with our differences and delusions. Only then it was easy to drop the barriers and get into the headspace of serving her to the best of my ability to fulfil her every need. We talked about strength in the past and the way people are able to sustain activities under difficult or trying circumstances. "You know where that comes from", my mother would say, referring to the All-Powerful, Omnipotent God. I am pretty sure that adrenaline may have been indicative of that, too.

In hindsight I can see now that my mum has always been my biggest supporter even if she didn't always appear to be, no matter how well or how badly I did. I finally understand I have been accepted for who I am. She has accepted the choices I have made. She has made peace with me, too.

I realise now: we are not that different. I am at peace now and I know that one thing is for sure: I will always keep the love alive.